IMPOSSIBLE™
THE COOKBOOK

IMPOSSIBLE™

THE COOKBOOK

HOW TO SAVE OUR PLANET, ONE DELICIOUS MEAL AT A TIME

Photography by Aubrie Pick

CHRONICLE BOOKS
SAN FRANCISCO

**This book is just the beginning.
Show us how you #CookImpossible and
you could end up in the next one.**

DEDICATED TO THE PEOPLE WHO
ACHIEVE THE IMPOSSIBLE

CONTENTS

This is a cookbook for people who love meat. Billions of people around the world depend on meat for its nutritional value and the daily pleasure it brings to their lives. But the way the world produces meat today has a devastating impact on the environment—greater than that of any other industry on Earth.

About one-third of all freshwater consumed on Earth goes toward animal agriculture. Raising animals for food has a greater negative impact on climate than the entire global transportation sector and is the primary cause of a catastrophic collapse of wildlife and biodiversity.

So we needed to find a way to produce the meat the world loves, while caring for our planet. And we did.

We're making meat—mouthwatering, craveable, nutritious meat—from plants, so we never have to use animals again. That way, we can eat all the meat we want, for as long as we want, without sacrificing the best planet in the known universe.

Hungry? Let's get cooking.

MISSION EARTH

By Pat Brown

CEO and Founder of Impossible Foods

People often ask me whether Impossible Foods is a tech startup or a food company. It's both. But more importantly, it's a *planet* company. Our real "product," the real measure of our success, is a thriving planet for future generations.

A TECHNOLOGY IN NEED OF CHANGE

Food has always been a collaboration between nature and science. For our entire history, humans have been exploring and experimenting with ingredients from nature, discovering which are safe, nutritious, and delicious, and finding endless ways to process, prepare, and combine them to create delicious foods that are more than the sum of the parts.

Since prehistoric times, animals have been the rudimentary technology we've used to transform plants into meat, fish, seafood, and dairy. Today, those foods are an important source of nutrition and pleasure for billions of people.

But as the demand for meat has surged, the dismal inefficiency of animals as a food-production technology has brought us to the verge of environmental catastrophe. Animal excrement and agricultural runoff have polluted about one-third of the rivers in America. The greenhouse-gas footprint of animal agriculture rivals that of every car, truck, bus, ship, airplane, and rocket ship combined.

Raising animals for food makes up the vast majority of the land footprint of humanity. All the buildings, roads, and paved surfaces in the world occupy less than 2% of Earth's land surface, and all the fruits and vegetables the world eats are grown on less than 1% of Earth's land. Grazing and growing feed crops for livestock, on the other hand, uses more than 45% of Earth's land.

And as the demand for meat continues to grow, so does its land footprint; forests are burning in the Amazon to clear land for cattle that's exported to other hemispheres. The global demand for meat, fish, and dairy foods is the primary driver of the ongoing, catastrophic collapse of diverse wildlife populations and ecosystems on land and in our oceans, rivers, and lakes. According to the World Wildlife Fund, the total number of wild mammals, birds, reptiles, amphibians, and fish living on Earth today is less than half what it was just 40 years ago—overwhelmingly due to the impacts of animal agriculture and overfishing.

Unless we can eliminate the use of animals as technology in the food system, we are racing toward ecological disaster. (In fact, of the 28,000 species at greatest risk of extinction, agriculture and aquaculture is listed as a key threat for 24,000 of them.) We need to act—now.

But expecting people to eliminate, or even reduce, their consumption of the meat, fish and dairy foods they love is completely unrealistic.

We're not going to solve this problem by pleading with consumers to eat beans and tofu instead of meat and fish. We need a solution.

WHAT IF THERE'S A BETTER WAY?

The truth is, people don't love meat, fish, and dairy *because* they come from animals. They love these foods *in spite of the fact* that they come from animals. Until today, the only technology they've known that can turn plants into the meat they love has been animals. So meat lovers have accepted the raising, exploitation, and slaughter of animals as a necessary evil. We asked the simple question, what if it weren't necessary after all?

In 2011, nobody was seriously working on this problem—the most important and urgent problem in the world. So, I quit my dream job as a biochemistry professor at Stanford University School of Medicine to found Impossible Foods.

We began in 2011 with a hypothesis: By understanding in molecular detail what makes meat delicious, we could deliberately choose specific ingredients from plants that match specific components of meat—and then we could transform them into meat that outperforms the best beef from a cow—in sustainability, cost, nutritional value, flavor, texture, craveability, and even "meatiness."

PEOPLE DON'T LOVE MEAT, FISH, AND DAIRY BECAUSE THEY COME FROM ANIMALS. THEY LOVE THESE FOODS IN SPITE OF THE FACT THAT THEY COME FROM ANIMALS.

SCIENCE + NATURE = FOOD

We started by building the best team of scientists and engineers ever to make delicious, nutritious meat from plants, not animals. We recognized that we didn't yet know how to do it, or what toolkit of plant ingredients we would need. We would have to discover the answers.

Our team approached the challenge of creating better meat with the same blend of creativity and concentration, and many of the same tools and techniques, that biomedical scientists use to understand how our bodies work and to discover treatments for previously incurable diseases. First, start with the hard fundamental research required to understand the basic principles and molecular mechanisms responsible for the flavors, aromas, textures, and juiciness that make meat delicious and craveable.Then, discover scalable plant sources of the specific proteins and other nutrients required to reproduce the magic of meat.

Our R&D team spent a half-decade exploring and experimenting before we launched our product to the public. Frankly, our early prototypes were terrible. (Our flavor team once compared an early prototype burger to rancid polenta!) But that's the way innovation works: Over several years, our product got better and better. More and more people began preferring Impossible™ Burger to one made from cows—and our results keep improving. The cow does not.

PLANTS ARE THE FUTURE

We started with the Impossible Burger because beef production is the most environmentally destructive segment of the livestock industry, and ground beef is a popular and iconic staple in America. Meanwhile, our team is also hard at work on plant-based pork, chicken, fish, cheese, and eggs. We're confident that the best meat and dairy products will soon come from plants, using the know-how and tools Impossible Foods is developing today.

The switch to a sustainable food system isn't just necessary and urgent. It's inevitable, and it's already happening. Over the next decade, all of the foods we now make from animals will begin to be replaced by plant-based counterparts that outperform them in every way that matters to consumers—taste, nutrition, and value—and trounce them in sustainability.

Today's Impossible Burger requires approximately 87% less water and 96% less land to produce, and its production generates about 89% lower greenhouse gas emissions than a conventional burger from cows.

THE CHEF CONNECTION

As we tested prototypes, we put our product to the ultimate test: We gave it to renowned chefs to try in their kitchens. They didn't just love it—they were excited to serve it in their restaurants. So, with very limited supply, we debuted in 2016 in the award-winning restaurants of David Chang, Traci Des Jardins, Tal Ronnen, and Chris Cosentino. They helped us send a powerful message that great meat doesn't have to come from animals.

Now chefs all over the world embrace Impossible Burger, which is available in about 20,000 restaurants throughout the United States and Asia. We're working relentlessly to make Impossible Burger meat available wherever animal meat is sold, including grocery stores, so people everywhere can enjoy it at home. We hope this book inspires you to experiment and create your new favorite meat dishes—with zero compromise to taste, nutrition, or the planet.

Dr. Patrick O. Brown is the CEO and founder of Impossible Foods and a former pediatrician, professor emeritus at the Stanford University School of Medicine, and cofounder of the Public Library of Science. Brown was elected to the United States National Academy of Sciences and the National Academy of Medicine and is a fellow of the American Association for the Advancement of Science.

EAT WELL, SAVE THE PLANET

Compared to beef, Impossible Burger has a tiny environmental footprint.

96% LESS LAND

87% LESS WATER

89% LESS EMISSIONS

Source: Quantis 2019 Impossible Burger 2.0 Comparative LCA Report

A CHEF'S PERSPECTIVE

By Traci Des Jardins
James Beard Award–winning Chef
and Restaurateur

I was first approached about the Impossible Burger in 2015 by a dear friend and business partner. He's someone who is always on the cutting edge, and when he talks, I always listen. What he described to me—a delicious, satisfying, plant-based meat—was something I couldn't begin to conceive of.

So, I hopped in my car and drove down to the headquarters of Impossible Foods in Redwood City, where, in a cramped conference room, I watched a guy in a business suit cook up a burger for me on a little plug-in griddle.

Still skeptical, I took a bite and couldn't quite comprehend what I had just seen and what I was eating. My eyes and mind had perceived what looked like ground beef sizzling and turning from red to brown with an unmistakable Maillard reaction, as the little conference room filled with the familiar aromas of cooking meat. And as I chewed, the flavor, the bite, the umami, and, well, the "beefiness" of beef were all right there.

It honestly took me about a month and a half of thinking about this and trying to absorb what it might mean for the world of food—and the world at large—to want to fully engage with what I had experienced.

That day I also was able to meet Pat Brown and hear from him why he had set out to create this incredible "meat made from plants." Clearly,

he was (and is) on a mission to save the world from the effects of its insatiable hunger for animal products. He made compelling and deeply intelligent and informed arguments about why the world needs plant-based alternatives.

I also toured the research lab at Impossible Foods and saw a room full of scientists hard at work. With a small test kitchen and loads of highly sophisticated equipment, Impossible Foods was doing things that we chefs can only do with our noses, our taste buds, and our limited powers of observation.

While cooking for people who only wanted plant-based options has never been my crusade, I have always been environmentally minded when making choices about what I wanted to present to the world as a chef. And I have many colleagues who feel the same way. As chefs, we know many passionate, environmentally conscious ranchers, fishermen, and farmers, and there are some inspired solutions out there for sure. But scale is a problem for so many of these solutions. The possibilities of what I had just seen seemed endless, and scale was part of the strategy from the moment the Impossible Burger was a nascent dream. So, I decided to get involved.

When I first tried Impossible Burger meat, it had already come quite a long way—the team had been working on it for over five years—and it was almost ready for prime time. My task was to help figure out what to do next. What changes could the product still benefit from? How might chefs and consumers react to it? Were there issues with how it cooked and performed? And how would this affect the cooking and eating experience? I strategized with the team and we decided that launching in restaurants with chefs who were well informed about the product would be a smart way to put our best foot forward.

While the development team continued to iterate, I reached out to my colleagues to introduce them to Impossible Foods. I must say I was apprehensive about how they might react. I remember telling a New York chef friend of mine about this plant-based meat. She paused, looked at me, and said, "Have you been in San Francisco too long and completely lost your mind?"

But she trusted me enough to meet with me, and a week later, we cooked up some of the Impossible Burger I had brought along. And the rest is history. She, like almost every chef I cooked it for—including myself—was blown away. As we went forward and introduced it to more and more chefs, we gathered great fans and an enthusiastic audience ready to help us debut this amazing stuff.

In my thirty-five years of cooking, this is the most *revolutionary* product I have encountered. I am proud to be one of the very first chefs to cook the Impossible Burger and serve it to the public. It's been a wild ride, starting with the crowds lining up outside Jardinière to be among the first to taste an Impossible Burger. It was fun and exciting, and the launch was met with tremendous enthusiasm. Sure, there were skeptics and naysayers who didn't want to like it, but mostly we experienced lots of very happy meat-eaters who quickly became huge fans.

Now that the Impossible Burger is available in stores, the avid home chefs, backyard grillers, and everyone else who wants to try their hand at cooking with it finally can, and we're launching this collection of recipes to celebrate. By now, chefs all over the world have shown us how versatile the Impossible Burger can be, and this book is brimming with their ideas and inspirations. Turns out, this plant-based wonder cooks just like ground beef. Have a blast with these recipes and experiment with your own. Best of all, enjoy cooking a product that's delicious, nutritious, and great for our planet. That's truly a dream come true.

IN MY NOW 35 YEARS OF COOKING, THIS IS THE MOST REVOLUTIONARY PRODUCT I HAVE ENCOUNTERED.

MEAT MADE FROM PLANTS

HOW'S THAT POSSIBLE?

A NEW APPROACH

Plant-based meat alternatives have been around for years, always with the same approach: Combine a bunch of ingredients to approximate the taste and texture of meat. We knew we needed to follow a completely different path. So we began at the end and worked backward, starting with the question, "What is meat, and what makes it so tasty?"

We decided that the only way to make meat from plants—meat that looks, feels, and tastes like animal-based meat—would be to "deconstruct" it at the molecular level and figure out how to replicate all of the components that give it the texture, flavor, aroma, and sizzle we know and love.

Then we found ways to source all of those components from the world of plants. You can check out what the Impossible Burger is made of on pages 22 to 23.

HEME: THE "MAGIC INGREDIENT"

One of our earliest and most important discoveries was that the key ingredient responsible for the unique flavors and aromas of meat—from either plants or animals—is heme.

Heme is an iron-containing molecule that occurs naturally in every cell of every animal and plant on the planet. It's an essential building block of life, most familiar as the molecule that carries oxygen in your blood. Heme is superabundant in animal muscle, and it's what makes meat uniquely delicious.

The fact is, you just can't make meat without heme. So, we figured out how to make heme from plants. The major source of heme in meat is the protein myoglobin. The roots of soybean plants contain a functionally identical protein called leghemoglobin.

But digging up soybean plants to harvest heme is neither efficient nor sustainable. So we took DNA from soy plants and inserted it into genetically engineered yeast. We ferment this yeast in tanks, in a process similar to what you'd find in a brewery. But instead of producing alcohol, our yeast cells multiply and produce heme.

The heme in the Impossible Burger is identical to the heme humans have been consuming for hundreds of thousands of years in conventional meat. It delivers the unique taste and iron content of beef, using a tiny fraction of the natural resources. And it's safety-verified by some of America's top food-safety experts and peer-reviewed academic journals.

Like the heme in animal meat, our heme interacts with the nutrients and minerals in the Impossible Burger as it cooks. It browns and "bleeds," and its flavor actually changes from raw to cooked, just like meat from animals.

Now you know how and why we do what we do. Where do you fit in? That's easy. By cooking, sharing, and eating the Impossible Burger, with a little help from this cookbook.

← HEME

POTATO
PROTEIN
↓

⌐ FAT

↑
MEAT
MADE FROM
PLANTS

SOY
PROTEIN →

↑
BINDERS

OUR RECIPE.
FROM EARTH, WITH LOVE.

Protein
Soy and potato proteins give the Impossible Burger the meaty texture and essential nutrition of ground beef.

Fat
Coconut and sunflower oils give the Impossible Burger its juicy richness and sizzle.

Binders
Methylcellulose (a culinary binder commonly found in ice cream, sauces, and jams) brings all the ingredients together.

Heme
Heme is a protein cofactor found in all living things that makes meat taste like meat.

A note on nutrition
The Impossible Burger has as much bioavailable iron and protein as ground beef from cows. Compared to a 4-oz [113-g] serving of "80/20" ground beef—which has 80 mg cholesterol, 23 g total fat, and 290 calories—Impossible Burger meat has 0 mg cholesterol, 14 g total fat (8 g of which are saturated fat), and 240 calories.*

The Impossible Burger is made with no animal hormones or antibiotics. And it's high in iron, thiamin, niacin, vitamin B6, folate, vitamin B12, and zinc. It's also a good source of potassium, riboflavin, phosphorus, and calcium—with seven times more calcium than 80/20 beef.

Nutritional information for the Impossible Burger is correct as of January 1, 2020, and is subject to change as product innovation continues. Visit www.impossiblefoods.com/burger for current information.

A word about genetically modified ingredients
Genetic engineering is an essential part of our mission and our product. We've always embraced the responsible, constructive use of genetic engineering to solve critical environmental, health, safety, and food security problems. We wouldn't be able to make a product that rivals or surpasses beef on every front—flavor, texture, nutrition, sustainability, versatility and accessibility—without it. The Impossible Burger is made with two key genetically engineered ingredients: heme (soy leghemoglobin)—the "magic" molecule that makes meat taste like meat—and soy protein sourced from farms in the Midwest that meets the highest standards of health, safety, and sustainability.

COOKING
THE
IMPOSSIBLE™

A USER'S GUIDE

HELPFUL HINTS

If you've ever cooked with ground beef, you already know how to cook with the Impossible Burger. Here are a few tips to get you started. You've got this.

Expect less shrinkage

When you cook a typical ground beef patty, it usually shrinks by 20 to 30 percent as it cooks. Impossible Burger meat shrinks 10 percent or less, which means you should make patties just about the size you want them to be when served. You might also be familiar with the technique of shaping ground beef patties with an indentation in the surface to make room for them to swell and expand as they exude fat and moisture. With the Impossible Burger there's no need to do this. The shape you start with is the shape you'll end up with.

Prepare it straight out of the fridge

Impossible Burger meat is easiest to handle when it's well chilled. Cook it straight from the refrigerator for best results.

Preheat for the perfect sear

Proper searing will give you the best flavor and texture. When cooking patties, preheat your open-flame grill to 425° to 450°F [215° to 230°C], oil the grates well, and cook the meat over direct heat. If you're using a skillet, preheat it over medium-high heat, add a little oil to the pan, and when it starts to shimmer, add the meat. You may want to reduce the heat to medium during cooking, depending on your stove, your pan, and the thickness of your patty.

Cook to medium-rare or medium

The texture and flavor of Impossible Burger meat will vary depending on how long you cook it. We recommend cooking patties to medium-rare or medium. Note that Impossible Burger meat cooks a bit faster than ground beef.

When cooking burgers in a preheated skillet, grill, or broiler, plan for 2 to 3 minutes per side for a 4-oz [113-g] patty (1 to 2 minutes per side for sliders and thinner patties)—just until you get a nice sear on the outside surfaces.

You can also use an instant-read thermometer to gauge doneness. Insert the thermometer lengthwise into the patty until the tip reaches the center of the meat.

Temperatures to look for: rare: 130°F [54°C], medium-rare: 135°F [57°C], medium: 140°F [60°C], medium-well: 145°F [63°C]; and well-done 160°F [71°C].

RARE
130°F [54°C]

MEDIUM
140°F [60°C]

WELL-DONE
160°F [71°C]

> ## "I ALWAYS ENJOY WHEN I SERVE IMPOSSIBLE TO SKEPTICS AND THEY SAY, 'NO WAY. THIS CAN'T BE MADE FROM PLANTS.'"
>
> —Chef Douglas Keane

IMPOSSIBLE BURGER MEAT IN ACTION

Formed: Meatballs, patties, and meatloaf

Just like you would with any ground meat, it's best to handle Impossible Burger meat lightly. It's often helpful to premix seasonings and other ingredients and then mix them into the meat just until everything is combined. Shape meatballs, patties, and meat loaf gently. If you're adapting a favorite meatball or meat loaf recipe that calls for eggs and you want to leave them out, you'll find that Impossible Burger meat binds beautifully without them. That said, keeping the eggs in your recipe can add flavor and richness and can give the dish a lighter texture.

Crumbling and sautéing

No difference from ground beef here. Just preheat the pan, add a little oil, crumble Impossible Burger meat into the pan, and stir to break up the meat until it browns. Add whatever seasonings you like, stir, and cook for a few more minutes.

Fillings

Use Impossible Burger meat to stuff ravioli, dumplings, and pastries, just as you would use ground beef.

Braising, soups, and sauces

When you're cooking Impossible Burger meat to make sauces, chilis, and soups, be aware that it tends to absorb a bit more liquid than ground beef. Making a favorite ground beef recipe? You may need to add up to 25 percent more liquid. We recommend browning Impossible Burger meat in the pan before adding the liquid ingredients. Because it doesn't release as much fat and moisture as beef during cooking, there's no need to drain excess liquid after browning. And keep in mind that Impossible Burger meat doesn't usually take as long to braise as conventional beef.

Baking and roasting

Bake or roast Impossible Burger meat in an oven just like ground beef. We suggest oven temperatures between 350°F [180°C] and 400°F [200°C].

HANDLING TIPS

Storage

Store Impossible Burger meat in your fridge. It'll keep for up to ten days unopened or three days once you open the package. If you don't use the full package, you can transfer any leftover meat to a resealable plastic bag, press out as much air as possible to prevent oxidation, then seal and store it in the fridge.

Freezing and thawing

Freeze Impossible Burger meat just as you would ground beef. Freeze it in its original package, or if you're freezing the unused portion of an opened package, transfer the meat to a resealable freezer bag and press out as much air as possible before sealing and freezing.

Impossible Burger meat thaws somewhat more slowly than ground beef. Thaw it in the refrigerator for 12 to 24 hours. Don't thaw at room temperature or under warm water. If you're in a hurry, you can thaw Impossible Burger meat in your microwave, using the defrost setting for small increments of time until the meat is thawed but still cold.

Safety and sanitation

Treat Impossible Burger meat just like any ground meat. Prep it on a clean work surface with clean hands and keep it refrigerated until you're ready to use it.

"THE FIRST TIME YOU COOK WITH WITH IT, IT'S INCREDIBLE TO WATCH HOW IT TURNS FROM RED TO BROWN."

—Chef Tal Ronnen

CHAPTER 1
STARTERS

IMPERIAL ROLLS

CHEF TRACI DES JARDINS

"Vietnamese imperial rolls are some of my very favorite things," says chef Traci Des Jardins, "and Impossible Burger meat makes a better filling than the classic pork and shrimp mixture, because it doesn't leak and make the wrappers soggy." These can be frozen and can go directly from the freezer into the frying oil. "If batch cooking is your thing," Traci says, "freeze a stash, and they'll be ready to fry and enjoy at a moment's notice." Look for wrappers that contain only rice, water, and salt without added tapioca starch, which makes them extra sticky.

1 oz [30 g] dried bean thread noodles (cellophane noodles)

12 oz [340 g] Impossible Burger

1 carrot, peeled and finely chopped

2 shallots, minced

4 cloves garlic, divided, minced

4 oz [115 g] shiitake mushrooms, stemmed and julienned (1¼ cups)

4 Tbsp [60 ml] coconut aminos, divided

2 Tbsp soy sauce, divided

Kosher salt and ground black pepper

1 bunch cilantro

Eighteen 8-in [20-cm] rice paper rounds

Vegetable oil, for frying

1 bird's-eye chile, stemmed and minced

1 Tbsp brown sugar

Juice of 2 limes

12 romaine lettuce leaves

1 bunch fresh mint

Soak the noodles in boiling water until soft, about 20 minutes. Drain well, then cut into 1-in [2.5-cm] pieces, adding them to a large bowl. Crumble the Impossible Burger into the bowl and add the carrot, shallots, 3 cloves garlic, mushrooms, 2 Tbsp aminos, 1 Tbsp soy sauce, ½ tsp salt, and some pepper. Finely chop half of the cilantro and add it to the bowl. Stir to mix completely.

To form the rolls, line a baking sheet with plastic wrap. Fill a wide, shallow bowl with hot water. Using a damp cutting board as a work surface, dip one rice paper round into the bowl of water to soften, 10 to 15 seconds. Remove the round from the water and place on the cutting board (to help absorb excess moisture before frying). Spoon about 3 Tbsp of the filling into a cigar-shaped mound in the center of the rice paper. Fold 2 opposite ends over the filling and roll tightly into a cylinder. Transfer to the prepared baking sheet. Repeat to form 18 rolls. Do not stack the rolls or allow them to touch or they will stick together.

In a large, deep skillet over medium-high heat, warm 2 to 3 in [5 to 7.5 cm] oil until hot but not smoking, about 325°F [165°C] on a deep-fry thermometer. Set a wire rack in a baking sheet and place next to the skillet.

While the oil heats, make the dipping sauce. In a bowl, whisk together the remaining 2 Tbsp aminos, 1 Tbsp soy sauce, and 1 clove garlic. Add the chile, brown sugar, and lime juice. Add ¼ cup [60 ml] water to thin the mixture to taste.

Make the garnish plate by arranging the lettuce, mint, and cilantro on a platter. Set aside.

Fry the rolls in batches to avoid crowding, turning with tongs, until golden brown, about 4 to 6 minutes. Transfer the rolls to the wire rack to drain, then transfer to a serving platter. Place the bowl of dipping sauce on the platter alongside the rolls. Using kitchen shears, cut each roll into 3 pieces. To eat, wrap each piece in a lettuce leaf with the mint and the cilantro sprigs and dip into the sauce.

MAKES 18 ROLLS; SERVES 6 TO 8

IMPOSSIBLE MOROCCAN CIGARS

CHEF TAL RONNEN

Tal Ronnen, chef/owner of the popular plant-based Mediterranean restaurant Crossroads Kitchen in Los Angeles, grew up in Israel, where his Moroccan Jewish nanny, Sol, cooked almost every meal he ate until he was eight years old. He loved it all, especially these crispy meat-filled treats that Sol whipped up in huge batches for weddings, bar mitzvahs, and parties. Today, Tal's version is one of the most popular appetizers on his menu. "This is really her recipe," he says, "but I adapted it to work with Impossible Burger meat, which gets a fantastic texture when you purée it to make the filling." Sol made her own *brik* dough, but Tal gets great results with Chinese spring roll wrappers. Look for thin pale-yellow wheat-flour wrappers, sometimes called spring roll skins. What you *don't* you want here are either Chinese egg roll wrappers, which tend to be too thick, or Vietnamese rice-flour spring roll wrappers.

SPICED FILLING

1½ tsp ground Aleppo pepper

1½ tsp ground cumin

1½ tsp ground black pepper

1 tsp sweet paprika

¾ tsp kosher salt

½ tsp ground turmeric

⅛ tsp cayenne pepper

1½ tsp butter, or plant-based butter spread

1 shallot, minced

8 cloves garlic, minced

12 oz [340 g] Impossible Burger

FLAVORED OIL

¼ cup [60 ml] vegetable oil

1 cup [155 g] chopped shallots

5 cloves garlic, chopped

1 Tbsp harissa paste

¼ tsp kosher salt

¼ tsp ground black pepper

¼ tsp red pepper flakes

1 Tbsp fresh lemon juice

1 Tbsp chopped fresh flat-leaf parsley

Vegetable oil, for frying

10 wheat-based Chinese spring roll wrappers, each about 6.5 in [16.5 cm] square

¼ cup [60 ml] plain yogurt or plain unsweetened almond milk yogurt

A day before you plan to make the cigars, prepare the spiced filling. In a small bowl, whisk together the Aleppo pepper, cumin, black pepper, paprika, salt, turmeric, and cayenne. In a large skillet over medium heat, melt the butter. Add the shallot, garlic, and spice mixture, stirring to combine. Cook until soft and fragrant, 3 to 5 minutes. Remove from the heat and let cool completely.

Crumble the Impossible Burger into a large bowl and add the cooled butter mixture. Mix until well combined, then transfer to a food processor and process into a smooth paste. Transfer to an airtight container and refrigerate overnight until well chilled.

To make the flavored oil, in a large skillet over medium-high heat, warm the oil. Add the shallots, garlic, harissa, salt, black pepper, and pepper flakes and cook, stirring, until fragrant, about 2 minutes. Remove from the heat and let cool. Stir in the lemon juice and parsley. Set aside.

CONT. NEXT PAGE

Add 1½ to 2 in [4 to 5 cm] vegetable oil to a large, heavy skillet and heat over medium-high heat until the oil is hot but not smoking (about 350°F/180° C) on a deep-fry thermometer.

While the oil is heating, assemble the cigars. Transfer the cold Impossible Burger filling to a pastry bag with ½-inch-wide tip. Fill a small bowl with warm water and place it next to your work station. On a work surface, cut the spring roll wrappers in half diagonally so you end up with two stacks of triangles. Place a damp kitchen towel over the wrappers to keep them from drying out. Working with one triangle at a time, arrange the wrapper with the central point facing up.

Pipe the filling lengthwise across the wrapper about 1 inch [2.5 cm] from the bottom edge to about 1 inch [2.5 cm] from the top edge. Fold each side of the bottom of the triangle over the mixture and, using the palm of your hand,

roll the pastry and filling toward the point into a tight cylinder. Dip your finger in the warm water and wet the inside tip of the triangle point to help seal the cigar. Set aside on a baking sheet. Repeat to use all of the filling and wrappers.

Line another baking sheet with paper towels. When the oil is hot enough, fry the cigars in batches, turning occasionally, until golden brown all over, 3 to 4 minutes. Using a wire skimmer, transfer the cigars to the paper towel–lined baking sheet to drain. Repeat to fry all the cigars.

To serve, arrange the cigars on a serving plate. Put the yogurt in a shallow bowl and top with the flavored oil. Serve the yogurt mixture alongside the cigars for dipping.

MAKES 15 CIGARS; SERVES 6 TO 8

"IMPOSSIBLE BURGER HAS CHANGED THE GAME FOR PLANT-BASED PROTEIN. FROM RAW HANDLING TO COOKING IN ANY APPLICATION, IT'S A TRUE ONE-TO-ONE REPLACEMENT FOR GROUND BEEF."

Chef J Michael Melton,
Head of Culinary,
Impossible Foods

PICADILLO EMPANADAS

CHEFS MARY SUE MILLIKEN AND SUSAN FENIGER

At the Border Grill restaurants in Los Angeles and Las Vegas, chefs Mary Sue Milliken and Susan Feniger serve empanadas with all kinds of fillings. "They're like lovely little packages with surprise gifts inside," says Mary Sue. "We love how Impossible Burger meat works with the sweet-savory flavors of our picadillo filling, which also makes a perfect stuffing for roasted poblano chiles." The easy cream cheese dough is rich, with a tender crumb, and it's very forgiving to work with. Mary Sue and Susan fill it with all kinds of sweet and savory fillings. You can even use it to make jam-filled cookies.

CREAM CHEESE EMPANADA DOUGH

- 8 oz [230 g] cream cheese or plant-based cream cheese, at room temperature
- ¾ cup [170 g] unsalted butter or plant-based butter spread, at room temperature
- ½ tsp kosher salt
- 2 cups [255 g] all-purpose flour

PICADILLO

- 1½ Tbsp olive oil
- 12 oz [340 g] Impossible Burger
- 1 yellow onion, finely chopped
- 6 Tbsp [70 g] coarsely chopped raisins
- 6 Tbsp [70 g] coarsely chopped pitted green olives
- 2 cloves garlic, minced
- ¾ tsp ground cumin
- ¾ tsp kosher salt
- ¾ tsp ground black pepper
- ½ tsp dried Mexican oregano
- 2 Roma tomatoes, seeded and diced
- 1 large egg beaten with 1 Tbsp milk, or 2 Tbsp vegetable oil

To make the dough, in the bowl of a stand mixer fitted with the paddle attachment, combine the cream cheese, butter, and salt and beat on medium speed until fluffy, 1 to 2 minutes. Add the flour slowly and mix just until a dough forms. Flatten the dough into a disk, wrap in plastic wrap, and refrigerate until chilled, at least 1 hour or up to 2 days.

To make the picadillo, in a skillet over medium heat, warm ½ Tbsp of the olive oil. Crumble the Impossible Burger into the pan and let brown undisturbed for 1 minute, then stir occasionally to brown on all sides without cooking all the way through, about 2 minutes. Transfer to a bowl and set aside.

Add the remaining 1 Tbsp oil to the pan, then add the onion. Cook, stirring, until slightly golden, 5 to 7 minutes. Add the raisins, olives, garlic, cumin, salt, pepper, and oregano. Cook until fragrant, 2 to 3 minutes. Reduce the heat to low, stir in the tomatoes, and cook, stirring occasionally, until the tomatoes break down and the onion starts to caramelize, 10 to 15 minutes. Return the Impossible Burger to the pot and cook, stirring, until the flavors are blended, about 5 minutes. Taste and adjust the seasoning, then remove from the heat and let cool completely.

On a lightly floured surface, roll the dough into a round about ⅛ inch [4 mm] thick. Using a 4-inch [10-cm] round cutter (or an upturned drinking glass and a paring knife), cut out as many rounds as you can. Press the dough scraps together, re-roll, and continue to cut

CONT. NEXT PAGE

out rounds until you use all of the dough; you should have 21 dough rounds. Refrigerate the dough for 15 minutes if it becomes too soft to work with. Let the dough rest for 5 minutes.

Place a generous 2 Tbsp of the filling in the center of each dough round. Brush the outer edge of half the dough round with the egg wash (or water), fold the other side over, and press the edges together to seal.

To crimp the edges, starting at one end of an empanada, pinch a corner of the dough and push it up toward the center of the half-round. Continue pinching and pushing the entire way around the half-round until you reach the opposite end of the empanada. Alternatively, crimp the edges by pressing the prongs of a fork along the edge of the half-round.

Transfer to a large parchment paper–lined baking sheet and repeat with remaining dough and filling; you should have 21 empanadas. Refrigerate the empanadas for 30 minutes or up to 12 hours, or freeze in an airtight container for up to 1 month. You don't have to defrost frozen empanadas before baking. (Cover and refrigerate the remaining egg wash if not baking the empanadas the same day.)

Preheat the oven to 400°F [200°F]. When the oven is ready, brush the pastries all over with the remaining egg wash or oil and arrange in a single layer on two baking sheets. Bake until golden brown, 15 to 20 minutes. Serve warm.

MAKES 21 EMPANADAS; SERVES 8 TO 10

DUTCH CROQUETTES (BITTERBALLEN)

MARJORIE MUNNEKE

There's nothing bitter about these crispy, golden one-bite wonders. They're a classic bar snack in the Netherlands, and their name refers to the flavor of the beer or bitters-spiked cocktails they're often served with. Impossible Burger meat really shines in fried applications like this one, with a springy chew that perfectly balances the crunchy bite of the crust. A sturdy brown mustard is the standard accompaniment for *bitterballen*, but if you're feeling fancy, try them with chef Andrei Soen's Special Sauce (page 124), Chimichurri (page 42), or a blend of Dijon mustard and mayo. Any way you go, you're in for a Dutch treat.

1½ Tbsp unsalted butter or plant-based butter spread

2 Tbsp all-purpose flour

Kosher salt and ground black pepper

¾ cup [180 ml] whole milk or vegetable broth

1 Tbsp vegetable oil, plus more for for deep-frying

12 oz [340 g] Impossible Burger

2 tsp finely chopped fresh flat-leaf parsley

¾ tsp curry powder (optional)

⅛ tsp ground nutmeg

¾ cup [85 g] fine dried bread crumbs

2 large eggs (optional)

Brown mustard, for serving

In a medium saucepan over medium heat, melt the butter. Whisk in the flour, 1 tsp salt, and a few turns of black pepper until a smooth roux forms. Gradually whisk in the milk. Bring to a boil, then reduce the heat to low and simmer, stirring constantly, until thickened, about 2 minutes.

In a skillet over medium heat, warm the 1 Tbsp oil. Crumble the Impossible Burger into the skillet and cook, stirring to break up the meat until browned, about 4 minutes. Add the meat to the sauce, then stir in the parsley, curry powder (if using), and nutmeg. Let cool, then cover and refrigerate until well chilled, about 1 hour.

Have ready a rimmed baking sheet. Put the bread crumbs into a shallow bowl. Scoop 1 Tbsp of the meat mixture and, using wet hands, shape the mixture into 1-in [2.5-cm] balls; you should have about 25 balls. Roll the balls in the bread crumbs to coat them evenly, then transfer to the baking sheet, cover, and refrigerate for 1 hour. If using eggs, set the remaining bread crumbs aside (otherwise save for another use and proceed with frying).

If using eggs, in another shallow bowl, beat the eggs with 1 Tbsp water. Dip each ball into the egg mixture and then coat evenly with the bread crumbs. Return to the baking sheet.

Line a platter with paper towels and set near the stove top. Fill a saucepan 2 to 3 inches [5 to 7.5 cm] full with oil and place over medium-high heat. Heat the oil to 400°F [200°F] on a deep-fry thermometer. Without overcrowding the saucepan, fry the croquettes, turning occasionally with a slotted spoon so they cook evenly, until golden brown, about 2 to 3 minutes. Using the slotted spoon, transfer the croquettes to the prepared platter. Serve hot, with the mustard alongside for dipping.

MAKES 4 TO 6 SERVINGS

CHURRASCO SKEWERS WITH CHIMICHURRI

CHEF J MICHAEL MELTON

If you're craving the smoke and char of churrasco-style steak, we've got you covered. It's as simple as grilling thin patties of lightly salted Impossible Burger meat and whipping up a fresh green chimichurri sauce to drizzle on top. Our chef, J Michael Melton, who has served these skewers to glowing reviews, recommends forming the patties first, then skewering them—it's easier than trying to shape the patties around the skewers. You can also skip the skewers altogether and form the mixture into larger oblong patties to grill and serve on toasted steak rolls. If you have leftover chimichurri, mix it with a little plant-based mayo and you've got a killer spread for burgers and sandwiches.

CHIMICHURRI SAUCE

- ½ cup [20 g] loosely packed finely chopped fresh flat-leaf parsley
- ¼ cup [10 g] loosely packed finely chopped fresh oregano
- ¼ cup [10 g] loosely packed finely chopped fresh cilantro
- 6 cloves garlic, minced
- ⅓ cup [80 ml] red wine vinegar
- 4 tsp sambal oelek (chile paste)
- ½ tsp kosher salt
- 6 Tbsp [90 ml] extra-virgin olive oil

- 1½ lb [680 g] Impossible Burger
- Kosher salt and ground black pepper
- ½ cup [60 g] shaved French breakfast radishes, for garnish (optional)
- ¼ cup [30 g] shaved Peppadew peppers or pimiento peppers for garnish (optional)

Soak twelve 8-in [20-cm] wooden skewers in water for at least 1 hour, up to overnight. Or have twelve metal skewers ready.

To make the chimichurri sauce, in a medium bowl, whisk together all of the ingredients except the oil. Slowly add the oil while whisking constantly, until well combined. Taste and adjust the seasoning; set aside.

To make the skewers, crumble the Impossible Burger into a large bowl and season with 1 tsp salt, mixing with your hands until well combined. Divide the Impossible Burger into 6 equal portions (about 2 oz/55 g each). Form each portion into a long, skinny cylindrical shape around one wooden skewer. Transfer to a small baking sheet. Season each skewer with black pepper.

Prepare a grill for direct cooking over high heat (450°F/230°C). Brush the grill grates clean. Grill the skewers, turning once or twice, until browned, about 1 minute per side. Transfer to a serving platter.

Whisk the chimichurri, then drizzle over the skewers. Garnish with the radishes and peppers (if using) and serve at once.

MAKES 4 TO 6 SERVINGS

ALBONDIGAS SOUP

CHEFS MARY SUE MILLIKEN AND SUSAN FENIGER

"Just about every culture has their version of meatball soup, and this," laughs chef Mary Sue Milliken, "is our version of Mexico's version. We like to make the meatballs small, so you get these wonderful explosions of flavor as you're eating." As soups go, this is a quick one to make, without the usual hours of simmering. And with the meatballs and all the vegetables, it's a great meal on its own. If you are serving it as part of a dinner party, Mary Sue suggests starting with a salad like a Tijuana-style Caesar or escarole and frisée with cheese and toasted pepitas. The meatballs also make a nice party nibble on their own, browned in a skillet, speared with tooth-picks, and served warm with a roasted-tomato salsa.

ALBONDIGAS

12 oz [340 g] Impossible Burger

¼ cup [10 g] finely chopped fresh cilantro

1 large egg, beaten, or 1 flax egg made from 1 Tbsp ground flaxseeds and 3 Tbsp water

1 tsp kosher salt

1 tsp ground black pepper

⅓ cup [20 g] fresh bread crumbs

3 Tbsp olive oil

1 small leek, white part only, thinly sliced

2 small carrots, peeled and cut into half-moons

Kosher salt and ground black pepper

¼ head cabbage, cored and cut into large chunks

1 jalapeño chile, seeded and thinly sliced

3 Roma tomatoes, seeded and diced

8 cups [2 L] vegetable broth

2 to 3 Tbsp white vinegar

To make the albondigas, in a large bowl, mix together the Impossible Burger, cilantro, egg, salt, and pepper. Add the bread crumbs and mix just until combined. Wet your hands and use your palms to roll into 1½-in [4-cm] meat-balls, then place on a baking sheet; you should have about 16 meatballs. Cover in plastic wrap and refrigerate until chilled, at least 30 minutes or up to 1 day.

In a 5-quart enameled Dutch oven over medium heat, warm the oil. Add the chilled meatballs in batches and brown on all sides, shaking the pot to prevent sticking, about 2 minutes. Using a slotted spoon, transfer the meatballs to a plate and set aside.

Add the leek and carrots to the pot, season with 1 tsp salt and a few turns of black pepper, and cook until the vegetables have started to soften, 2 to 4 minutes. Add the cabbage, jalapeño, and tomatoes and cook, stirring frequently, until the vegetables are soft, about 3 minutes longer. Pour in the broth. Bring to a boil, reduce the heat to a simmer, and add the meatballs. Simmer, uncovered, until the meat-balls are cooked through, about 10 minutes. Stir in the vinegar, then taste and adjust the seasoning. Serve hot.

Variation: *For a heartier dish, add a handful or two of cooked rice or uncooked small-shaped pasta when you add the broth.*

MAKES 4 SERVINGS

CHILI CHEESE FRIES

CHEF J MICHAEL MELTON

If you're a fan of perfect, crispy French fries, try chef J Michael Melton's restaurant-style technique. He coats the sliced potatoes with a dusting of cornstarch and then fries them twice. "It's worth the extra step," says J Michael. "The first fry cooks the interior of the potato so it's soft and creamy, and the second fry crisps the exterior beautifully. Plus, fries made this way keep their heat and texture longer, even when you pile on the chili and cheese sauce." This chili recipe requires only minimal prep and comes together in under an hour. It's also great over rice or corn chips.

CHILI

1 Tbsp vegetable oil

½ yellow onion, finely chopped

2 cloves garlic, minced

12 oz [340 g] Impossible Burger

1 Tbsp chili powder

2 tsp paprika

1½ tsp ground cumin

1 tsp ground coriander

¼ tsp cayenne

Kosher salt

One 14 oz [400 g] can crushed tomatoes

1 cup [240 ml] vegetable stock

FRIES

2½ lb [1.2 k] russet potatoes, peeled and cut into ¼ in [6 mm] thick fries

3 Tbsp cornstarch

Vegetable or peanut oil, for frying

Kosher salt

½ recipe Plant-Based Whiz (page 89)

1 cup sour cream, cilantro lime crema (page 70), or plant-based sour cream

3 green onions, white and green parts, thinly sliced

To make the chili, in a pot over medium-high heat, warm the oil. Add the onion and garlic and cook, stirring, until the onions soften, about 3 minutes. Crumble the Impossible Burger into the pot and cook, stirring to break up the meat, until browned and cooked through, about 4 minutes. Stir in the spices and ½ tsp salt. Add the tomatoes and stock. Bring the mixture to a boil, then reduce the heat to medium-low and simmer until thickened, about 30 minutes. Remove from the heat and cover to keep warm while you make the fries.

To make the fries, line a large baking sheet with paper towels. In a colander, rinse the potatoes well with cold water. Drain well, spread on the baking sheet, and blot as dry as you can.

Put the cornstarch in a wide bowl, add the potatoes, and toss until coated evenly. Arrange the potatoes on a clean baking sheet in one layer.

Fill a large heavy pot one-third full of oil. Line another large baking sheet with paper towels. Over high heat, warm the oil to 325° to 350°F [165° to 180°C] on a deep-fry thermometer. Carefully add the potatoes to the hot oil in batches to avoid overcrowding. Turn the potatoes occasionally with a slotted spoon or tongs and fry, until the outside of the potatoes form a slight crust, about 4 minutes.

Transfer the potatoes to the prepared baking sheet, arrange them in a single layer, and season with salt. Let cool for 20 minutes or up to 2 hours.

Reheat the oil over high heat to 350°F to 360°F [180° to 182°C] on a deep-fry thermometer. Fry the potatoes, turning occasionally, until golden brown and crisp, about 5 minutes. Transfer the fries to the prepared baking sheet, arrange them in a single layer, and season with salt.

To assemble, re-warm the chili. Transfer the hot fries to a platter. Top with the chili, plant-based whiz, sour cream, and green onions. Serve.

MAKES 4 TO 6 SERVINGS

ASIAN LETTUCE WRAPS

CHEF J MICHAEL MELTON

"Of all the Impossible recipes I make for people," says our Head of Culinary, chef J Michael Melton, "this one gets the most enthusiastic response." It's a mash-up of Asian cuisines and inspirations based on his time working in some of the Bay Area's top restaurant kitchens. The meat simmers in a Japanese yakitori-style sweet-hot *tare* sauce and then gets spooned onto lettuce leaves and topped with pickled vegetables borrowed from *banh mi*. "This is one of those combos where the whole is way greater than the sum of the parts," says J Michael. He recommends using living lettuce (the kind sold with the roots still attached), because it tends to have the most perfectly uniform leaves. You can serve these as appetizers or starters, or go family-style and pass around a bowl of the meat filling with a big platter of leaves and pickled vegetables on the side.

PICKLED VEGETABLES

1 large carrot, peeled and julienned (about 1 cup/125g)

½ small daikon, peeled and julienned (about 1 cup/125 g)

1 cup [240 ml] rice wine vinegar

¼ cup [50 g] sugar

SEASONED MEAT

½ cup [120 ml] rice wine vinegar

5 Tbsp [90 g] sambal oelek (chile paste)

3 Tbsp soy sauce

3 cloves garlic, minced

1-in [2.5-cm] piece fresh ginger, peeled and minced

1½ tsp ground five-pepper blend or black pepper

1 cup [200 g] packed dark brown sugar

2 Tbsp vegetable oil

12 oz [340 g] Impossible Burger

1 head Bibb or butter lettuce, leaves separated (12 to 14 leaves)

½ English cucumber, halved lengthwise, seeded, and thinly sliced crosswise into crescents

½ cup [20 g] chopped fresh cilantro

½ cup [20 g] chopped fresh mint

½ cup [20 g] chopped fresh Thai basil

1 lime, cut into wedges

To make the pickled vegetables, toss together the carrot and daikon in a medium heatproof bowl. In a small saucepan over medium-high heat, bring the vinegar and sugar to a boil, stirring until the sugar dissolves. Pour the vinegar mixture over the vegetables, stir to combine, then let stand until slightly pickled, at least 1 hour. Pour the leftovers into a mason jar, seal, and refrigerate for up to 1 month.

To make the seasoned meat, in a saucepan over medium-high heat, stir together the vinegar, sambal oelek, soy sauce, garlic, ginger, and pepper and bring to a boil. Remove from the heat and stir in the brown sugar until it dissolves. Set aside.

In a skillet over medium-high heat, warm the oil. Crumble the Impossible Burger into the skillet and cook, breaking it up with a spoon until it browns, about 4 minutes. Stir in the vinegar mixture, reduce the heat to medium, and simmer until the liquid reduces and thickens, about 8 minutes. Remove from the heat and let the meat cool for 5 minutes.

To assemble, spoon 2 to 3 Tbsp of the Impossible Burger mixture into each lettuce leaf. Top each with some of the pickled vegetables and cucumber. Garnish with the chopped herbs, then serve, accompanied by the lime wedges.

MAKES 4 TO 6 SERVINGS

PAN-FRIED CHIVE DUMPLINGS

CAROLYN CHEN

Impossible Burger meat is spot-on in fried, steamed, or baked dumplings, because it binds beautifully and takes on just the right chewy texture. And here's another thing: With the right seasonings and flavors, it can speak the language of just about any cuisine. In these classic Chinese-style dumplings, ingredients like ginger, green onions, garlic, soy sauce, and sesame oil help make that magic happen.

DIPPING SAUCE

1 Tbsp soy sauce

1 Tbsp rice vinegar

1 green onion, white part only, minced (about 1 Tbsp)

3 cloves garlic, minced (about 1 Tbsp)

1 tsp sugar

1 tsp vegetable oil

Chili oil, red pepper flakes, or hot sauce to taste (optional)

DUMPLINGS

12 oz [340 g] Impossible Burger

¾ cup [30 g] finely chopped fresh chives

2 tsp peeled and grated ginger

2 tsp minced green onion, white and green parts

2 tsp rice vinegar

2 tsp soy sauce

2 tsp toasted sesame oil

1 clove garlic, minced

¾ tsp cornstarch

Pinch of ground white pepper

24 dumpling wrappers

Vegetable oil, for frying

To make the dipping sauce, whisk together all of the ingredients in a bowl. Set aside.

To make the dumpling filling, in a large bowl, stir together all the ingredients until well combined.

To form the dumplings, have ready a small bowl of water. Place a dumpling wrapper in the palm of your hand. Scoop 1 Tbsp filling into the center of the wrapper. Dip your index finger into the water and lightly wet the edge of the wrapper all the way around. Fold in half, but don't seal the edges shut.

To create ribbon-like folds, start at one end of the dumpling and make small pleats on the half of the wrapper closest to you all the way around the crescent until you get to the other end, pushing with your dominant thumb and pinching with the index finger and thumb of your other hand as you go. Use additional water to seal if needed. Set aside on a baking sheet and repeat with the remaining dumplings. You should have 2 dozen dumplings.

Add a thin layer of oil to a large nonstick skillet and heat over medium-high heat. In batches, add enough dumplings to the pan so they fit in a single even layer without crowding. Cook until the dumplings are golden brown on the bottom, about 1 minute.

Add 2 Tbsp water to the pan and immediately cover the skillet to steam the dumplings. Let the dumplings steam until the water evaporates, about 1 minute, then repeat adding the water and letting it evaporate twice more. Remove the cover and let the dumplings crisp, about 30 seconds. Using cooking chopsticks or a metal spatula, transfer to a serving dish and serve hot, with the dipping sauce. Repeat to cook all of the dumplings.

MAKES 2 DOZEN DUMPLINGS; SERVES 6

TACO SALAD

CHEF TRACI DES JARDINS

"The taco salads of my youth were ground beef sautéed with taco seasoning mix, canned beans and chiles, orange cheese, iceberg lettuce, lackluster tomatoes, and maybe some avocado," says chef Traci Des Jardins. "In this version, I've elevated it all just a bit, bringing in toasted guajillos and pumpkin seeds, Oaxaca cheese, homemade tortilla chips, and Little Gem lettuce to make the salad special. If access to ingredients is a challenge, you can always revert back to any of those old-school options. Except for the ground beef."

PICKLED ONION AND ROASTED POBLANO

½ red onion, thinly sliced

½ tsp kosher salt

¼ cup [60 ml] red wine vinegar

1 poblano chile

TACO MEAT

2 guajillo chiles, seeded

4 Tbsp [60 ml] vegetable oil

½ red onion, finely chopped

2 cloves garlic, minced

½ tsp dried oregano, preferably Mexican

2 tsp ground cumin

1 Tbsp ancho chile powder

1 tsp ground coriander

1 tsp kosher salt

12 oz [340 g] Impossible Burger

BEANS

One 15-oz [430 g] can pinto beans, drained and rinsed

2 Tbsp extra-virgin olive oil

¼ cup [10 g] chopped fresh cilantro

Kosher salt and ground black pepper

AVOCADO-LIME DRESSING

2 ripe avocados, halved, pitted, and peeled

1 jalapeño chile, seeded if desired

Juice of 2 limes

¼ cup [60 ml] mayon-naise or plant-based mayonnaise

¼ cup [10 g] fresh cilantro leaves

1 tsp kosher salt

Leaves from 2 heads Little Gem lettuce or 1 head romaine, cut into strips ½ in [12 mm] wide

1 basket cherry tomatoes, halved (optional)

4 green onions, white and pale green parts, thinly sliced

1½ cups [45 g] fresh cilantro leaves

4 radishes, thinly sliced

4 oz [115 g] Oaxaca cheese, pulled into strips, or 1 cup (115 g) shredded plant-based cheese

¼ cup [30 g] pumpkin seeds, toasted

2 cups [60 g] fried tortilla strips or chips, preferably homemade

CONT. NEXT PAGE

To make the pickled onion, put the onion in a small bowl and toss with the salt. In a small saucepan over medium-high heat, bring the vinegar and ¼ cup [60 ml] water to a boil. Pour over the onion, then set aside for 30 minutes.

To make the roasted poblano chile, using tongs, roast the chile over an open flame on the stove top, turning until blackened all over, 8 to 10 minutes. Put into a zip-top plastic bag to steam for about 5 minutes to help loosen the skin. Rinse under water and remove all charred skin, seeds, and the stem. Cut the chile into thin strips and set aside.

To make the taco meat, using kitchen shears, cut the guajillo chiles into very fine strips about ⅛ in [3 mm] wide. Line a plate with two paper towels and set it next to the stove top. In a medium skillet over medium-high heat, warm 2 Tbsp of the oil. Add the guajillo strips and cook until crisp, 30 seconds to 1 minute. Using a slotted spoon, transfer to the paper towels to drain, leaving the oil in the pan.

Add the chopped onion, garlic, spices, and salt to the skillet. Cook over medium-low heat, stirring, until the onion is golden, 8 to 10 minutes. Scrape the mixture into a bowl and set aside. Add the remaining 2 Tbsp oil to the skillet and increase the heat to medium-high. Crumble the meat into the skillet and cook, stirring occasionally to break it up, until browned and cooked through, 5 to 6 minutes. Return the onion mixture to the skillet and stir until well combined. Remove from heat and set aside.

To make the beans, drain the pickled onions and transfer half of the onions to another bowl to reserve for garnish. Add the beans and olive oil to the remaining onions, then the poblano strips and chopped cilantro. Season to taste with salt and pepper. Mix well and set aside.

To make the avocado-lime dressing, add the avocados, jalapeño, mayonnaise, lime juice, cilantro, salt, and ¼ cup [60 ml] water to a food processor and blend to a smooth purée. Transfer to a small bowl and set aside.

To assemble, in a large bowl, toss together the lettuce, tomatoes (if using), green onions, half of the cilantro leaves, and half of the dressing, adding more if necessary to lightly dress the vegetables. On a large platter or individual plates, spoon the remaining dressing and spread into a large round, then top with the taco meat and the marinated beans and onions. Top with the lettuce mixture, then garnish with the radishes, cheese, remaining cilantro, pumpkin seeds, reserved pickled onions, reserved guajillo strips, and tortilla strips.

MAKES 6 SERVINGS

" I LIKED IMPOSSIBLE BURGER FROM THE MINUTE I SAW THE SCIENCE BEHIND IT. I KNEW THAT SET IT APART FROM THE OTHERS."

Chef Sarah Schafer

JAMAICAN PATTIES WITH CALYPSO SAUCE

CHEF KWAME ONWUACHI

If someone says "beef patty" in Jamaica, chances are they're not talking burgers. Throughout the Caribbean, a *patty* is a hand pie with a flaky pastry crust and a savory curried-meat filling. "This is the first dish I ever made with Impossible Burger meat," says chef Kwame Onwuachi, "and I became a believer, because it worked perfectly and tasted great the first time!" He serves the patties with his own homemade calypso sauce, the classic sweet-tangy hot sauce of Jamaica. If you're pressed for time, buy yourself a bottle to use on everything and anything.

DOUGH

2½ cups [320 g] all-purpose flour

1 Tbsp ground turmeric

1½ tsp kosher salt

1 cup [190 g] vegetable shortening

½ cup ice water

FILLING

1½ Tbsp vegetable oil

½ yellow onion, finely chopped

12 oz [340 g] Impossible Burger

1½ Tbsp Jamaican jerk paste

2 tsp Jamaican curry powder

1 tsp kosher salt

CALYPSO SAUCE

1 Tbsp grapeseed oil

½ yellow onion, chopped

1 yellow bell pepper, seeded and chopped

1 habanero chile, stemmed and finely chopped

5 cloves garlic, minced

1 cup [240 ml] carrot juice

2 Tbsp cane vinegar or rice vinegar

½ Tbsp sugar

½ tsp kosher salt

To make the dough, add the flour, turmeric, and salt to a food processor. Pulse a few times to combine, then add the shortening and ice water. Pulse until a ball of dough forms. On a floured surface, press the dough into a disk, wrap in plastic wrap, and refrigerate until well chilled, at least 4 hours or up to 24 hours.

To make the filling, in a medium saucepan over medium heat, warm the oil. Add the onion and cook, stirring, until translucent, about 3 minutes. Crumble the Impossible Burger into the pan, then add the jerk paste, curry powder, and salt. Cook, stirring to break up the meat, until the mixture is cooked through and browned, about 10 minutes. Taste and adjust the seasoning, then set aside to cool to room temperature. Cover and refrigerate until chilled, about 1 hour.

To make the calypso sauce, in a small saucepan over medium heat, warm the oil. Add the onion and cook, stirring, until translucent, about 3 minutes. Add the bell pepper and cook, stirring, until it begins to soften, about 3 minutes. Add the chile and cook, stirring for about 3 minutes. Add the garlic, carrot juice, vinegar, sugar, and salt. Bring to a boil, then reduce the heat to a simmer and cook, stirring occasionally, until the liquid has reduced to a syrup, about 30 minutes. Transfer to a blender and purée until smooth. Taste and adjust the seasoning. Transfer to a serving bowl and set aside.

Preheat the oven to 400°F [200°C] and line two baking sheets with parchment paper. Have a small bowl of water ready.

On a floured work surface, roll the dough to a thickness of ⅛ in [4 mm]. Using a 3-in [7.5-cm] round cutter, cut out as many rounds as you can—you should have about 30 rounds. Press the dough scraps back together and continue rolling and cutting until all the dough is used.

Place 1 Tbsp filling in the center of each round. Dip your finger into the water and wipe it around the edge of the round to help seal. Fold the dough over the filling and seal the edges with a fork, pressing out any air from the center. Repeat to fill all of the pastries. Transfer to the prepared baking sheets, spacing the pastries so they're not touching.

Bake until golden brown, about 15 minutes. Using a metal spatula, transfer to a wire rack. Serve hot, with the calypso sauce on the side for dipping.

MAKES 30 PASTRIES; SERVES 10

XINJIANG POCKETS

CHEF MAY CHOW

At Little Bao in Hong Kong, chef May Chow loves to reimagine Chinese favorites in fresh, casual-cool ways. She has always loved the crispy turnovers with a juicy spiced veal filling served at Islam Food, a popular halal/Chinese restaurant in Kowloon, one of Hong Kong's oldest neighbor-hoods. This is her plant-based take on those much-loved meat pockets.

DOUGH

2½ cups [320 g] all-purpose flour

1 tsp instant yeast

¾ tsp kosher salt

2 Tbsp vegetable oil

2 Tbsp maple syrup

CHILI POWDER MIX

½ tsp garlic powder

½ tsp ground black pepper

½ tsp hot paprika

½ tsp red chili powder

½ tsp ground cumin

½ tsp kosher salt

½ tsp sugar

¼ tsp white sesame seeds

FILLING

1 Tbsp cumin seeds

6 Tbsp [40 g] Chinese pickled daikon rad-ish, finely chopped

1 green onion, white and green parts, finely chopped

1 recipe Chili Powder Mix (above)

12 oz [340 g] Impossible Burger

2 Tbsp vegetable oil

To make the dough, in the bowl of a stand mixer fitted with the paddle attachment, stir together the flour, yeast, and salt on low speed just until well combined. Slowly add ¾ cup plus 3 Tbsp [210 ml] water, the oil, and maple syrup. Mix on medium-low speed until the dough is well combined and smooth, about 5 minutes.

Grease a rimmed baking sheet. Divide the dough into 11 equal pieces (1¼ oz/35 g each). Cover with a kitchen towel and set aside in a warm place until doubled in size, about 1 hour.

Meanwhile, make the chili powder. In a bowl, whisk together all of the ingredients.

To make the filling, in a skillet over medium-low heat, toast the cumin seeds until darkened, about 5 minutes. Transfer to a cutting board and coarsely chop. Transfer to a large bowl and add the daikon, green onion, 2 Tbsp water, and chili powder mix and whisk to combine. Crumble the Impossible Burger into the bowl and mix the ingredients until well combined.

Divide the mixture into 11 equal-sized portions (1¼ oz/35 g each), then form each into a ball. Place the balls on a rimmed baking sheet, cover with plastic wrap, and refrigerate until the meat is firm, at least 30 minutes or up to 1 day.

On a lightly floured work surface, roll out each piece of dough into a 3-inch [7.5-cm] round. Add a ball of filling to the center of the round, then fold the dough edges up and over the meat to conceal it. Pinch the seams together to seal. Turn over the pocket and, using the rolling pin, gently flatten it into a round about ½ inch [12 mm] thick. Return the pockets to the baking sheet and refrigerate until ready to panfry.

In a nonstick skillet over medium heat, warm the oil. In batches to avoid overcrowding, panfry the pockets, turning once, until golden brown and heated through, 2 to 3 minutes per side. Serve hot. The cooked pockets can be refrigerated in an airtight container for up to 1 day or frozen for up to 3 weeks. To reheat, panfry hot pockets over medium-low to medium heat.

MAKES 11 HOT POCKETS; SERVES 4 TO 6

SOUTHEAST ASIAN STUFFED FLATBREADS (MURTABAK)

WINNIE YEOH

These flatbreads—filled with seasoned meat and eggs and browned on a griddle—are popular street-food snacks in Malaysia, Singapore, and Indonesia, where they're often served with sliced cucumbers and a curry sauce for dipping. Here, the easy no-cook sauce has just the right mix of sweet, hot, tangy, and curry-licious flavors to complement the rich, meaty filling. It's best to make the sauce an hour or more before serving so all those flavors can bloom and blend.

HOT AND SOUR CURRY SAUCE

¼ cup [60 ml] rice wine vinegar

3 Tbsp tamarind concentrate

3 Tbsp sweet soy sauce

1 cup [40 g] chopped fresh cilantro

2 green onions, white and green parts, thinly sliced,

2 Tbsp sambal oelek (chile paste)

1 Tbsp peeled and grated ginger

2 tsp Madras curry powder

1 clove garlic, minced

Juice of ½ lime

DOUGH

3 cups [385 g] all-purpose flour

½ tsp kosher salt

1 Tbsp vegetable oil

FILLING

1 Tbsp vegetable oil

1 yellow onion, finely chopped

2 cloves garlic, minced

1 tsp peeled and grated fresh ginger

1½ lb [680 g] Impossible Burger

1 tsp chili powder

1 tsp ground coriander

1 tsp garam masala

1½ tsp kosher salt

¼ tsp ground turmeric

½ cup [120 ml] vegetable oil

2 large eggs, beaten (optional)

2 yellow onions, thinly sliced

To make the sauce, in a medium bowl, whisk together all of the ingredients until well combined. Cover and refrigerate for 1 day before serving for the best flavor.

To make the dough, in a large bowl, stir together the flour and salt. Slowly add 1 cup [240 ml] lukewarm water and the oil, stirring until well combined and the dough forms a ball. Turn the dough out onto a work surface and knead with your hands, until the dough becomes soft and pliable, 8 to 10 minutes. (Alternatively, mix the dough together in the bowl of a stand mixer using the dough hook attachment on low speed for 8 to 10 minutes.) Form the dough into a large ball, return to the bowl, and cover with plastic wrap. Set aside at room temperature and let the dough rest for at least 1 hour and up to 6 hours.

To make the filling, in a large skillet over medium heat, warm the oil. Add the onion and cook, stirring, until soft and translucent, about 3 minutes. Add the garlic and ginger and cook, stirring, until fragrant, about 1 minute. Crumble the Impossible Burger into the pan and cook, stirring to break up the chunks, until browned, about 5 minutes. Add the chili powder, coriander, garam masala, salt, and turmeric and stir to combine. Remove the pan from the heat and set aside to cool.

To assemble, divide the dough into 6 equal balls. Lightly coat each ball with oil. Using a rolling pin, roll each ball into a paper-thin 18-inch [46-cm] square.

Brush the center of each piece of dough with a layer of egg (if using), dividing it evenly among the dough squares and leaving a 1½-in [4-cm] border around the edge. Spoon about ¾ cup [170 g] of the meat mixture into the center of each dough piece. Top the meat mixture with the onions, dividing them evenly.

Fold two opposite sides of the dough over the meat mixture, overlapping them slightly, then fold the other two opposite sides over, again overlapping them slightly, to create a neat square that seals the meat mixture inside. Brush the top of each flatbread with about ½ Tbsp of the oil.

Heat a large nonstick pan or griddle over medium heat. Brush the pan with about ½ Tbsp of the oil. In batches if necessary, carefully transfer the flatbreads to the heated pan, oiled side down. Cook until golden brown on the bottom, 2 to 4 minutes. Brush the top of each flatbread with another ½ Tbsp of oil, then use a metal spatula to turn them and cook the second side until golden brown, about 2 minutes. Cut each flatbread into 4 or 6 pieces and serve hot, with the curry sauce.

MAKES 6 TO 12 SERVINGS

ETHIOPIAN SPICED MEAT WITH HUMMUS AND TOASTED CASHEWS

CHEF KWAME ONWUACHI

Sambusas are Ethiopia's version of samosas: pastry turnovers with a spiced meat filling. "There's a huge Ethiopian population here in DC," says chef Kwame Onwuachi, "and sambusas are a popular pre-service snack with our staff at Kith/Kin." That was his inspiration for this quick, easy recipe, in which he skips the pastry and serves a sambusa-style filling over creamy hummus. "Anyone can make this, and it's so flavorful," says Kwame. "The seasonings and the texture always remind people of ground lamb."

HUMMUS

One 15½-oz [445-g] can chickpeas, drained and rinsed

3 Tbsp fresh lemon juice

3 cloves garlic, chopped

2 tsp tahini (sesame paste)

1½ tsp ground cumin

¼ tsp kosher salt

⅓ cup [80 ml] extra-virgin olive oil

ETHIOPIAN SPICED MEAT

1½ Tbsp grapeseed oil

1 small white onion, finely chopped

8 cloves garlic, minced

2 tsp minced fresh ginger

1½ tsp berbere (Ethiopian spice mix)

¾ tsp ground cumin

¼ tsp ground cardamom

¼ tsp ground cinnamon

Kosher salt

12 oz [340 g] Impossible Burger

¼ cup [30 g] chopped toasted cashews

¼ to ½ cup [7 to 15 g] chopped fresh flat-leaf parsley leaves, according to taste

Extra-virgin olive oil, for serving

3 to 4 pita breads, warmed and cut into wedges, for serving

To make the hummus, add the chickpeas, lemon juice, garlic, tahini, cumin, and salt to a food processor and process until smooth. With the machine running, slowly add the olive oil until well combined. Taste and adjust the seasoning; set aside. You should have about 1½ cups [360 g].

To make the meat, in a large sauté pan over medium heat, warm the oil. Add the onion, garlic, ginger, berbere, cumin, cardamom, cinnamon, and ¼ tsp salt and cook, stirring, until the onion is translucent and the mixture is fragrant, about 10 minutes. Crumble the Impossible Burger into the pan and cook, stirring to break it up, until browned and cooked through, 8 minutes. Taste and adjust the seasoning.

To serve, spread the hummus onto a large dish, smoothing the top and creating a well in the center. Spoon the warm meat into the center of the hummus and garnish with the cashews, parsley, and a drizzle of olive oil. Serve with warm pita wedges alongside.

MAKES 6 SERVINGS

CHAPTER 2
ENTREES

THAI LAAB WITH FRESH HERBS

CHEF CHRIS COSENTINO

"Laab is a classic Thai dish of ground meat cooked in a wok at high heat, then mixed with flavorful herbs, Thai chilies, and vegetables," says chef Chris Cosentino. "It's always served with a wedge of cabbage to cool the palate." His Impossible version captures all the tastes and textures of the Thai original. "Fish sauce is one of the keys to authentic laab," he says. "If you want to keep things plant-based, try vegan fish sauce. You can find it online or in Vietnamese markets, and it'll take you all the way to true laab flavor."

8 cloves garlic

¾ tsp kosher salt

3 Tbsp vegetable oil

3 bird's-eye chiles, stemmed and minced

12 oz [340 g] Impossible Burger

¾ tsp red pepper flakes

¾ tsp Chinese five-spice powder

¾ tsp freshly grated nutmeg

¼ tsp ground coriander

¼ tsp ground cardamom

¼ tsp ground black pepper

2 Tbsp chopped fresh mint

1 green onion, white and green parts, sliced

1 Tbsp chopped fresh cilantro

1 Tbsp fish sauce or vegan fish sauce, or more to taste

2 makrut lime leaves, thinly sliced

2 Tbsp thinly sliced lemongrass, peeled white bulb only

½ cup [60 g] thinly sliced red onion

½ cup [85 g] halved cherry tomatoes

¼ cabbage, cored and separated into leaves

On a cutting board, smash the garlic cloves with the salt to make a paste using the flat side of a chef's knife; you should have just over 2 Tbsp.

In a large skillet over medium heat, warm the oil. Add the garlic paste and chiles and cook, stirring, until fragrant, about 2 minutes. Crumble the Impossible Burger into the pan and add the red pepper flakes, five-spice powder, nutmeg, coriander, cardamom, and black pepper and cook, stirring to combine and break up the meat as it browns, about 2 minutes. Stir in the mint, green onion, cilantro, and 1 Tbsp fish sauce and cook until the mixture is fragrant and some of the meat has charred, about 4 minutes.

Transfer the mixture to a large serving bowl. Toss with the lime leaves, lemongrass, red onion, and tomatoes. Taste and adjust the seasoning. Serve with cabbage leaves for scooping.

MAKES 4 SERVINGS

VIETNAMESE PHỞ

CHEF TRACI DES JARDINS

Can you really make legit phở without simmering a bunch of bones? "You can get amazingly close," says chef Traci Des Jardins. She gets all the umami of a beef bone broth from dried shiitake mushrooms, kombu (dried kelp), charred onions and ginger, and a powerful plant-based flavor booster: coconut aminos, a liquid made from fermented coconut palm nectar that makes a great substitute for fish sauce. "The Impossible meatballs complete the full phở effect," says Traci, "with just the right meaty taste and bouncy bite." Nothing faux about it.

BROTH

2 unpeeled yellow onions, halved

3-inch [7.5-cm] piece unpeeled fresh ginger, halved

2½ qt [2.4 L] vegetable broth

1 cup [30 g] dried shiitake mushrooms

4 whole cloves

4 star anise pods

1-inch [2.5-cm] cinnamon stick, preferably Vietnamese

1 piece kombu kelp (optional)

2 Tbsp coconut aminos, or more to taste

2 Tbsp soy sauce, or more to taste

MEATBALLS

12 oz [340 g] Impossible Burger

1 shallot, minced

2 tsp peeled and minced fresh ginger

1 clove garlic, minced

1 Tbsp soy sauce

1 Tbsp coconut aminos or soy sauce

1½ tsp sugar

½ tsp kosher salt

16 oz [455 g] fresh thin rice noodles, or 14 oz [400 g] dried rice stick noodles (*banh pho*)

2 cups [200 g] mung bean sprouts

1 bunch fresh Thai basil

½ bunch fresh cilantro

1 lime, cut into 4 wedges

1 jalapeño chile, thinly sliced

1 bunch green onions, white and green parts, thinly sliced

Hoisin sauce, for serving

Sriracha sauce, for serving

To make the broth, in a small cast-iron skillet over medium-high heat, cook the onions and ginger until blackened, about 20 minutes. Transfer the blackened onions and ginger to a stockpot and add the vegetable broth, mushrooms, cloves, star anise, cinnamon stick, and kombu (if using). Place over high heat, bring to a boil, then reduce the heat to low and simmer, covered, until the flavors have deepened, about 2 hours. Strain the broth through a fine-mesh sieve, discarding the solids, then transfer back to the stockpot. Season with the coconut aminos and soy sauce, adding more if necessary.

To make the meatballs, preheat the oven to 500°F [260°C]. Line a large rimmed baking sheet with aluminum foil. Crumble the Impossible Burger into a bowl and add the shallot, ginger, garlic, soy sauce, coconut aminos, sugar, and salt and mix with your hands until thoroughly combined. Scoop up 1 heaping Tbsp (about 1 oz/30 g) of the meatball mixture and form into balls about 1½ inch [4 cm] in diameter; you should have 16 balls. Place on the prepared baking sheet. Bake until browned on top, about 7 minutes. Transfer to a wire rack.

CONT. NEXT PAGE

To assemble the phở, rewarm the broth over medium-low heat until steaming. Taste and adjust the seasoning. While the broth is heating, prepare the noodles by bringing another large pot of water to a boil. If using dried noodles, soak them in hot water until slightly softened, 15 to 20 minutes, then drain. Separate the drained or fresh noodles into 4 portions (4 oz/115 g each). Working with one portion at a time, place the noodles in a noodle strainer or medium wire sieve and immerse in the boiling water until soft, 10 to 20 seconds. Drain over the boiling water and transfer to an individual soup bowl. Repeat with the remaining portions.

Add the bean sprouts to the pot and blanch for 30 seconds. Drain, run under cold water, and place on a large plate along with the basil, cilantro, lime wedges, jalapeños, and half of the green onions.

Add four meatballs to each soup bowl. Divide the remaining green onions among the bowls, then ladle the hot broth over the top. Serve at once with the plate of accompaniments and bottles or small bowls of hoisin and Sriracha alongside.

MAKES 4 SERVINGS

TOSTONES WITH PICADILLO

OLIVIA PEAR

The next time you cruise past the plantains—those large banana-like things you've probably been ignoring in the produce section—pick up a bunch to experiment with. Set aside your banana-based preconceptions and think potato or taro root. Plantains go from firm and starchy when green to sweeter when yellow. Tostones, made with green plantains, are fried, smashed, and then refried to create crispy golden disks you can treat and eat just like griddle-smashed potatoes. They're a perfect platform for picadillo, a Latin sweet-savory spiced meat dish. For a whole new way to nacho, try layering the picadillo with tortilla chips, Plant-Based Whiz (page 89), and pickled jalapeños.

PICADILLO

2 Tbsp olive oil

2 yellow onions, finely chopped

4 cloves garlic, minced

1½ lb [680 g] Impossible Burger

2 tsp kosher salt

Ground black pepper

4 ripe Roma tomatoes, chopped

2 Tbsp red wine vinegar

2 bay leaves

1 Tbsp ground cinnamon

1 Tbsp ground cumin

Pinch of ground cloves

Pinch of ground nutmeg

⅔ cup [120 g] golden raisins

⅔ cup [120 g] sliced pitted green olives

TOSTONES

Vegetable oil, for frying

2 green plantains, peeled and cut into slices 1 in [2.5 cm] thick

Kosher salt

¼ cup [10 g] chopped fresh cilantro, for garnish

To make the picadillo, in a large, heavy skillet over medium-high heat, warm the oil. Add the onions and cook, stirring occasionally, until they are golden and soft, about 10 minutes. Add the garlic and cook until fragrant, about 1 minute. Add the Impossible Burger and allow it to brown, breaking up the meat with a spoon as it does, about 4 minutes. Season with salt and a few turns of black pepper.

Add the tomatoes, vinegar, bay leaves, and spices and stir to combine. Reduce the heat to low, cover, and simmer, stirring occasionally, until the mixture is thick and fragrant, about 30 minutes. Stir in the raisins and olives and continue to simmer for 15 minutes.

Meanwhile, make the tostones. Heat 1½ in [4 cm] oil in a large, heavy skillet until hot but not smoking (about 350°F/180°C on a deep-fry thermometer). Line a baking sheet with parchment paper. Using a slotted spoon, add the plantains to the hot oil. Fry, turning once, until golden brown on both sides, 4 minutes total.

Transfer the tostones to the baking sheet in a single layer; keep the heat on. Lay another piece of parchment over the plantains and smash each with the back of a metal spatula to ¼ in [6 mm] thick. Return the plantains to the hot oil to fry again, turning once, until golden brown, about 5 minutes. Remove the parchment paper from the baking sheet and replace with paper towels. Transfer the tostones to the paper towels and sprinkle with salt.

On a large serving platter, serve the hot tostones topped with the picadillo, or spoon the picadillo into the center of the dish and fan the tostones around it. Garnish with the cilantro and serve at once.

MAKES 6 SERVINGS

THREE-BEAN CHILI WITH LIME CREMA

CHEF J MICHAEL MELTON

Attention chili-con-carne-vores: We promise you'll find this chili from our chef, J Michael Melton, just as meatily crave-worthy as the original Southwest-style classic. Serve it old-school with crackers or slabs of corn bread, or use it to build the best nachos ever. It also makes an awesome topping for hot dogs and burgers. (Impossible Burgers, obviously.)

1 Tbsp vegetable oil

1 yellow onion, finely chopped

1 carrot, peeled and diced

1 red bell pepper, seeded and finely chopped

1 green bell pepper, seeded and finely chopped

1 yellow bell pepper, seeded and finely chopped

2 stalks celery, finely chopped

2 jalapeño chiles, minced

4 cloves garlic, minced

Kosher salt

1½ lb [680 g] Impossible Burger

2 Tbsp chili powder

1 Tbsp ground cumin

2 tsp chipotle chile powder

2 tsp ground coriander

1 tsp sweet paprika

1 tsp cayenne

3 bay leaves

One 28-oz [875-g] can crushed tomatoes

2 cups [480 ml] vegetable broth

¼ cup [60 ml] apple cider vinegar

One 15-oz [430-g] can kidney beans, drained and rinsed

One 15-oz can [430-g] great northern beans, drained and rinsed

One 15-oz can [430-g] black beans, drained and rinsed

Ground black pepper

LIME CREMA

1 cup [240 ml] sour cream or plant-based sour cream

½ cup [20 g] loosely packed finely chopped fresh cilantro

Finely grated zest and juice of 1 lime

1 tsp kosher salt

In a stockpot over medium heat, warm the oil. Add the onion, carrot, bell peppers, celery, jalapeños, and garlic. Season with 1 tsp salt and cook, stirring occasionally, until softened, about 5 minutes. Crumble the Impossible Burger into the pot and cook, stirring to break it up, until browned and cooked through, about 3 minutes.

Add the chili powder, cumin, chipotle powder, coriander, paprika, cayenne, and bay leaves and stir to combine. Add the tomatoes, broth, and vinegar and stir to combine. Bring to a boil, then reduce the heat to medium-low and simmer, stirring occasionally, until the mixture has thickened and the flavors have deepened, about 30 minutes.

Stir in the beans, then cook until warmed through, about 5 minutes. Season with salt and pepper to taste.

While the chili simmers, make the lime crema. In a bowl, whisk together all of the ingredients. Set aside until ready to use, or cover and refrigerate for up to 5 days.

Ladle the chili into individual bowls, dollop each serving with 2 Tbsp crema, and serve hot.

MAKES 6 SERVINGS

"FOR ME AS A CHEF, IT'S THE CONSISTENT FLAVOR AND PERFORMANCE OF IMPOSSIBLE BURGER MEAT THAT REALLY MATTERS. YOU CAN'T GET THAT FROM BEEF."

Chef Tanya Holland

DROP BISCUITS WITH SPICED SAUSAGE GRAVY

CHEF TANYA HOLLAND

"I grew up spending summers in the South," says chef Tanya Holland, "and I still think of biscuits with sausage gravy as one of the homiest and most comforting of breakfasts." Her gravy recipe is tasty proof of a simple equation: Impossible Burger meat plus sausage seasonings equals . . . sausage! You can even form Tanya's sausage mixture into patties and brown them in a skillet to serve for breakfast. "My drop biscuits are really user-friendly," she says. "There's no rolling or cutting. In fact, the less you handle this dough, the better."

DROP BISCUITS

2 cups [340 g] all-purpose flour

2 tsp baking powder

¾ tsp kosher salt

1¼ cups [300 ml] whole milk or plant-based milk

4 Tbsp [55 g] unsalted butter or plant-based butter spread, melted

SAUSAGE GRAVY

1 tsp fennel seeds

1 tsp dried sage

1 tsp dried thyme

1 tsp packed light brown sugar

1 tsp kosher salt

¼ tsp ground black pepper

¼ tsp garlic powder

¼ tsp red pepper flakes

12 oz [340 g] Impossible Burger

3 Tbsp vegetable oil

¼ cup [30 g] all-purpose flour

2 cups [480 ml] whole milk or plant-based milk, plus more if needed

To make the biscuits, preheat the oven to 425°F [220°C]. Line a large rimmed baking sheet with parchment paper. In a large bowl, whisk together the flour, baking powder, and salt. Add the milk and butter and stir with a fork just until the dough comes together; it will be soft and wet (do not overmix).

Using two spoons, scoop six equal-sized portions (4 oz/115 g each) of the batter onto the prepared baking sheet, spacing them at least 1 in [2.5 cm] apart. Bake until the biscuits are golden brown and puffed, about 20 minutes. Set aside.

While the biscuits are baking, make the gravy. In a medium bowl, whisk together the fennel seeds, sage, thyme, sugar, salt, pepper, garlic powder, and red pepper flakes. Crumble the Impossible Burger into the bowl and mix together with your hands until thoroughly combined.

In a heavy skillet over medium-high heat, warm 2 Tbsp of the oil until hot but not smoking. Crumble the Impossible Burger mixture into the pan. Cook until browned, stirring with a wooden spoon to break up the Impossible Burger, 3 to 4 minutes. Reduce the heat to medium-low and stir in the remaining 1 Tbsp oil. Sprinkle the flour over the Impossible Burger mixture, stirring until it is absorbed. Slowly add the milk, stirring constantly, until well combined. Simmer until the gravy thickens, stirring occasionally, 3 to 4 minutes, then taste and adjust the seasoning. (If the gravy gets too thick, thin it with a little more milk.)

Carefully split open each warm biscuit and place it on an individual plate. Spoon hot gravy over the top, dividing it among the biscuits, and serve at once. (If the biscuits have cooled, split them, then toast cut side down in a buttered pan or in a toaster.)

MAKES 6 SERVINGS

TINGA TOSTADAS WITH PICKLED CILANTRO SLAW

CHEF J MICHAEL MELTON

Impossible Foods chef, J Michael Melton, created this saucy simmered tinga—a classic Mexican-style filling for tacos and tostadas—to show off the amazing braising talents of Impossible Burger meat. It absorbs the complex flavors of the sauce without overcooking, and just like any good braise, tastes even better the second day. J Michael serves it on tostadas with refried beans and a cabbage slaw that has an unusual twist: It's pickled! He grew up in a restaurant family in South Carolina, where this kind of slaw was a mainstay on the menu. "My folks called it ten-day slaw," he says, "because once you pickle it, it lasts forever. I like it because it's got a lot more going on in terms of taste and texture than your standard-issue slaw."

PICKLED SLAW

- ¼ head cabbage, cored and very thinly sliced
- ¼ yellow onion, finely chopped
- ½ red bell pepper, seeded and diced
- ½ yellow bell pepper, seeded and diced
- ¼ cup [50 g] sugar
- ¾ cup [180 ml] rice wine vinegar
- 2 Tbsp olive oil
- ½ tsp ground mustard
- 1½ tsp kosher salt
- ¼ cup [10 g] loosely packed chopped fresh cilantro

REFRIED BEANS

- 1 Tbsp vegetable oil
- ½ yellow onion, finely chopped
- 1 clove garlic, minced
- One 15-oz [430 g] can pinto beans, with liquid
- 1 tsp ground cumin
- 1 tsp ground coriander
- Kosher salt
- ¼ cup [60 ml] vegetable broth
- Juice of ½ lime
- Ground black pepper

TINGA

- 2 Tbsp vegetable oil
- ½ yellow onion, finely chopped
- 3 jalapeño chiles, seeded (or not) and minced
- 3 cloves garlic, minced
- 12 oz [340 g] Impossible Burger
- 1 Tbsp chili powder
- 1 Tbsp sweet paprika
- 1 tsp ground cumin
- 1 tsp ground coriander
- Kosher salt
- 1 cup [240 ml] vegetable broth
- One 14½-oz [455-g] can crushed tomatoes
- 3 Tbsp minced canned chipotles in adobo

- Eight 4-inch [10cm] corn tostada shells
- 2 avocados, peeled, pitted, and thinly sliced
- ½ cup [70 g] crumbled queso fresco or plant-based cheese (optional)
- 1 to 2 limes, cut into wedges

To make the slaw, put the cabbage in a large baking dish. Sprinkle the onion and peppers over the top in an even layer, then sprinkle with the sugar. In a small saucepan, stir together the vinegar, olive oil, mustard, and salt. Bring to a boil, then pour the pickling mixture over the cabbage mixture. Cover tightly with plastic wrap and set aside at room temperature until cooled completely. Drain the cabbage mixture and transfer to a bowl. Stir in the cilantro. Cover and refrigerate until ready to use.

To make the refried beans, in a saucepan over medium heat, warm the oil. Add the onion and garlic and cook until softened, about 3 minutes. Stir in the beans and their liquid, the cumin, coriander, ½ tsp salt, and the vegetable broth. Cook until fragrant and heated through, 5 to 7 minutes. Transfer the mixture to a food processor, reserving the saucepan. Process to a smooth purée, adding the lime juice as the machine is running. Season to taste with salt and pepper. Return the beans to the saucepan and cover to keep warm.

To make the tinga, in a large skillet over medium-high heat, warm the oil. Add the onion, jalapeños, and garlic and cook, stirring occasionally, until softened, 3 to 4 minutes. Crumble the Impossible Burger into the pan and cook, stirring to break it up, until browned, about 4 minutes. Add the chili powder, paprika, cumin, coriander, and ½ tsp salt and stir until fragrant, about 1 minute. Add the broth, tomatoes, and chipotle and bring to a simmer. Reduce the temperature to medium-low to maintain a steady simmer and cook, stirring occasionally, until reduced slightly and flavorful, 25 to 30 minutes. Taste and adjust the seasoning. Cover and keep warm over low heat.

To assemble the tostadas, preheat the oven to 350°F [180°C]. Put the tostadas on a baking sheet and heat in the oven for 3 to 4 minutes. Meanwhile, gently stir the beans over medium-low heat until warmed through.

Divide the tostadas among individual plates. Divide the beans among the tostadas, spreading them into an even layer. Top the beans with the tinga mixture, dividing it evenly. Top each tostada with pickled slaw, again dividing it evenly. Arrange one-fourth of an avocado on each tostada, then sprinkle with the queso fresco (if using). Serve each with a wedge of lime.

MAKES 4 TO 8 SERVINGS

CHILAQUILES WITH RED BEANS AND CHARRED TOMATILLO SALSA

CHEF SARAH SCHAFER

"This is a delicious and impressive brunch recipe that you can make for two or scale up to feed a crowd," says chef Sarah Schafer, who serves it at Irving Street Kitchen in Portland, Oregon. You can make the salsa and the chorizo mixture ahead of time, but wait until just before serving to brown the chorizo and assemble the chilaquiles. The chorizo is also great on its own. Just form the mixture (minus the beans) into patties and brown them in a skillet.

TOMATILLO SALSA

2 lb [900 g] tomatillos, husked and rinsed

1 red onion, cut into slices ½ in [12 mm] thick

1 or 2 jalapeño chiles

3 Tbsp chopped fresh cilantro

2 cloves garlic, coarsely chopped

Finely grated zest and juice of 1 or 2 limes

Kosher salt

TORTILLA CHIPS

Vegetable oil, for frying

One 16-oz [455-g] package corn tortillas, cut into ½-in [12-mm] strips

Kosher salt, for sprinkling

CHORIZO

12 oz [340 g] Impossible Burger

1½ Tbsp apple cider vinegar

2 Tbsp ground ancho chile

2 tsp kosher salt

1 tsp sweet paprika

½ tsp finely chopped fresh oregano

½ tsp ground coriander

¼ tsp ground black pepper

⅛ tsp ground ginger

⅛ tsp ground allspice

1 tsp vegetable oil

1 (15-oz) can pinto beans, drained and rinsed

Juice of 1 lime

½ cup [70 g] crumbled queso fresco or plant-based cheese

1 Tbsp vegetable oil (optional)

6 large eggs (optional)

1 diced white onion

1 Tbsp Mexican crema or plant-based sour cream

To make the tomatillo salsa, preheat a grill for direct cooking over high heat (450°F), or preheat a stove-top grill pan over medium-high heat. Grill the tomatillos, onion, and jalapeño(s), turning as needed, until deeply charred. (Small to medium tomatillos and jalapeños will take 13 to 18 minutes, while larger tomatillos and onion will take up to 25 minutes.) Let the vegetables cool slightly, then transfer to a blender with the cilantro, garlic, lime zest and juice, and ½ tsp salt. Purée until smooth, adding water to reach the desired consistency. Season to taste with salt. Set aside.

To make the tortilla chips, in a heavy pot over medium-high heat, warm 3 to 4 in [7.5 to 10 cm] oil until hot but not smoking, about 350°F [180°C] on a deep-fry thermometer. Line a baking sheet with paper towels. Working in two batches, add the corn tortilla strips and fry, turning often, until crisp and golden, about 6 minutes. Using a wire skimmer, transfer to paper towels to drain and sprinkle with salt.

Preheat the oven to 400°F [200°F].

CONT. NEXT PAGE

To make the chorizo, crumble the Impossible Burger into a large bowl. Add the vinegar and spices and mix well with your hands to combine. In a large cast-iron skillet over medium heat, warm the oil. Add the chorizo mixture and cook, stirring, until browned, about 6 minutes. Add the beans and the lime juice and stir to combine. Season to taste with salt. Cook, stirring, until warmed through and fragrant, about 5 minutes.

Pour 1½ cups [360 ml] of the tomatillo salsa into a medium bowl, add the chips, and toss to coat. Arrange the chips on top of the chorizo mixture. Bake until the chips have started to soften and are heated through. Carefully remove the skillet from the oven and sprinkle with the queso fresco. Bake until the cheese is warm, about 5 more minutes.

While the chilaquiles warm in the oven, prep the eggs (if using). In a skillet over medium heat, warm the oil. Add the eggs and fry for 1 minute, then turn and fry on the second side for 15 to 30 seconds for over easy and 1 minute for over medium.

Remove the chilaquiles from the oven. Scatter the onion over the top and drizzle with the crema. Top each portion with a fried egg (if using) and serve the remaining salsa on the side.

MAKES 6 SERVINGS

LASAGNA BOLOGNESE WITH ROASTED SQUASH

KIM LAIDLAW

"Lasagna can be a project," says our editor, the cookbook author and food writer Kim Laidlaw, "so I use a few shortcuts to make the job easier." She opts for crème fraîche instead of the traditional béchamel sauce, which saves time and adds a tangy flavor that balances the sweetness of the squash. And she uses no-boil noodles, which she loves as much for their convenience as for the way they retain their al dente texture. Kim notes that you can substitute fresh pasta sheets, which also don't need to be boiled. "I love the rich caramel flavor and creamy texture that roasted squash adds to lasagna," she says. "Kuri is my favorite, but just about any firm winter squash—like kabocha, butternut, acorn, or even sugar pie pumpkin—will work."

Bolognese Sauce (page 103), recipe doubled

½ cup [115 g] tomato sauce

ROASTED SQUASH

1 medium kuri, kabocha, or butternut squash (1½ to 2 lb [680 to 910 g]), peeled, seeded, and cut into ½-inch pieces

½ tsp red pepper flakes

Olive oil

Kosher salt and ground black pepper

1 cup [240 ml] crème fraiche or plant-based sour cream

1 cup [110 g] finely shredded Parmesan or plant-based Parmesan

1 lb [455 g] fresh mozzarella or plant-based mozzarella, thinly sliced

9 sheets no-boil lasagna noodles

Make the Bolognese sauce, adding the tomato sauce when you add the canned chopped tomatoes.

To roast the squash, preheat the oven to 425°F [220°C]. On a large rimmed baking sheet, toss the squash pieces with the pepper flakes, a drizzle of olive oil, and some salt and pepper. Roast the squash, turning once, until tender and browned, about 25 minutes.

To assemble and bake the lasagna, lower the oven temperature to 375°F. In a bowl, stir together the crème fraiche and ½ cup [55 g] Parmesan. Lightly oil a 9 by 13 in [23 by 33 cm] baking dish.

Spread a big ladleful of Bolognese sauce over the bottom of the pan. Place a layer of 3 lasagna noodles, then a layer of Bolognese sauce, half of the butternut squash, ⅓ of the crème fraiche mixture, ⅓ of the mozzarella, and then another layer of lasagna noodles. Repeat with a layer of Bolognese sauce, the remaining butternut squash, ½ the remaining crème fraiche, ½ the remaining mozzarella, and a final layer of lasagna noodles. Top with a layer of Bolognese sauce, the remaining crème fraiche, and the remaining mozzarella. Sprinkle with the remaining ½ cup [55 g] Parmesan.

Bake until bubbly and the pasta is tender, about 45 minutes. If the cheese starts to brown too much, cover the baking dish with aluminum foil. Let the lasagna rest for about 10 minutes before serving.

MAKES 8 SERVINGS

THAI BASIL STIR-FRY (PAD KA-PRAO)

JEN SHIU

Pad ka-prao, or "holy basil stir-fry," is the poster child of Thai street food. It's traditionally made with ground chicken, beef, or pork quickly cooked with chiles, garlic, seasonings, and a sacred secret ingredient: holy basil—a kind of Thai basil with a peppery licorice flavor. If you can find holy basil, by all means go for it. If you can't, Thai or Italian basil are both good substitutes. This quick stir-fry makes a satisfying weeknight one-dish meal, especially when you serve it over sticky rice or jasmine rice and top it with runny-yolked fried eggs.

3 Tbsp vegetable oil

2 Tbsp minced shallots

8 Chinese long beans, cut into 1-in [2.5-cm] pieces (about 1 cup/150 g)

3 garlic cloves, minced

1 bird's eye chile, thinly sliced

12 oz [340 g] Impossible Burger

1½ Tbsp Thai sweet soy sauce (*kecap manis*)

2 tsp soy sauce

2 tsp vegetarian fish sauce or coconut aminos (optional)

¾ cup [20 g] packed fresh holy basil leaves

4 large eggs (optional)

1 lime, cut into wedges

Steamed jasmine rice, for serving

In a well-seasoned wok over medium heat or a large skillet over high heat, warm 2 Tbsp of the oil. Add the shallots and stir-fry until golden brown, about 1 minute. Add the long beans, garlic, and chile and cook until the beans turn bright green and the mixture is fragrant, about 1 minute.

Increase the heat to high if using a wok and add the Impossible Burger, breaking it up with a spoon and allowing it to brown, 2 to 3 minutes. Add the soy sauces and fish sauce, if using, stir to combine, then reduce the heat to low. Stir in the basil and cook until just wilted.

If serving with fried eggs, heat a large nonstick skillet over medium-high heat and warm the remaining 1 Tbsp of oil. Crack the eggs into the pan and cook, covered, until the whites are cooked and the yolks are still runny, 1 to 1½ minutes.

Divide the rice among four individual bowls and spoon the Impossible Burger mixture over the top, dividing it evenly. Top each portion with a fried egg (if using) and serve at once, with the lime wedges on the side.

MAKES 4 SERVINGS

KOREAN BULGOGI WITH SPICY SCALLION PANCAKES

CHEF J MICHAEL MELTON

Our chef, J Michael Melton, came up with a way to recreate the taste and texture of Korean bulgogi beef by browning patties of Impossible Burger meat, dicing them, and then reheating them in a rich, umami-intense bulgogi sauce, sweetened, per tradition, with grated Asian pear. "This is a great example of how you can push the limits with Impossible Burger meat to refashion global favorites like bulgogi," says J Michael. "Serving this over rice would be the traditional go-to, but level-up to the scallion pancake for the win."

BULGOGI SAUCE

- 1½ cups [180 g] peeled, cored, and grated Asian pears (about 2 pears) or sweet apples, such as Fuji, Gala, or Red Delicious
- 7 Tbsp mirin
- 5 Tbsp tamari or soy sauce
- ¼ cup [50 g] packed dark brown sugar
- 3 Tbsp gochujang (Korean chili paste)
- 1½ Tbsp peeled and grated fresh ginger
- 2 Tbsp minced shallots
- 2 Tbsp toasted sesame oil
- 3 cloves garlic, minced
- 2 green onions, green and white parts, thinly sliced

SCALLION PANCAKES

- 1 cup [120 g] all-purpose flour
- 4 green onions, green parts only, cut into ½-in [12-mm] pieces
- 1 clove garlic, minced
- 2 tsp gochujang
- 1 tsp gochugaru (Korean red chili flakes)
- 1 tsp tamari or soy sauce
- ½ tsp kosher salt
- 1 large egg, lightly beaten

- 12 oz [340 g] Impossible Burger
- 2 Tbsp vegetable oil
- 5 green onions, white and green parts, thinly sliced
- 5 Tbsp toasted sesame seeds

To make the bulgogi sauce, in a bowl, whisk together all of the ingredients until well combined. Set aside.

To make the pancake batter, in a bowl, whisk together the flour, ½ cup [120 ml] water, the green onions, garlic, gochujang, gochugaru, tamari, and salt until well combined. Add the egg and whisk to combine. Set aside.

Divide the Impossible Burger into three equal portions and shape into patties ¼ in [6 mm] thick.

In a large, nonstick skillet over medium-high heat, warm 1 Tbsp oil. Sear the patties, turning once halfway through, until browned and cooked through, about 7 minutes. Transfer to a cutting board to cool completely. Wipe out the pan with a paper towel. Cut the patties into ½ in [12 mm] cubes.

To cook the pancakes, preheat the oven to 200°F [95°C]. Place a baking sheet in the oven. In the skillet over medium-high heat, warm 1 Tbsp oil. In batches to avoid overcrowding, add ¼ cup [60 ml] batter to the pan for each pancake. Cook, turning once, until golden brown, 4 to 6 minutes. (Add more oil if needed while cooking.) Transfer the pancakes to the baking sheet to keep warm; you should have 8 pancakes.

Reduce the heat to medium-low and add the sauce to the skillet. When it comes to a boil, add the meat. Stir until warm, about 3 minutes.

To assemble, divide the pancakes between 4 plates. Top each with the bulgogi, dividing it evenly. Garnish with green onions and toasted sesame seeds. Serve at once.

MAKES 4 SERVINGS

GYROS WITH GREEK SALAD, TZATZIKI, AND GRILLED PITAS

CHEF DOUGLAS KEANE

Even though he's Irish American, this is one of chef Douglas Keane's favorite childhood comfort foods, because he grew up in Detroit, where gyros are a Greektown staple. "I still love a good old-style gryo," he says, "but I have to say, I like this version even better. It's moister and fresher tasting than the usual smashed, seared, and sliced gyro meat." Rather than blending in seasonings, Douglas likes to treat all ground meat (including the kind made from plants) with a light hand. So he forms unseasoned patties and sprinkles them with the seasoning just before cooking.

TZATZIKI SAUCE

½ cup [120 ml] whole-milk Greek yogurt or plant-based Greek yogurt

2 Tbsp finely chopped fresh dill

1 clove garlic, minced

1 Tbsp red wine vinegar

¼ tsp kosher salt

⅛ tsp sugar

GREEK SALAD

1 cup [170 g] cherry tomatoes, halved (quartered if large)

1 cup [155g] finely diced cucumber (about ½ seeded cucumber)

¼ cup [50 g] thinly sliced pepperoncini

2 Tbsp thinly sliced red onion

2 Tbsp chopped pitted Kalamata olives

3 Tbsp crumbled feta cheese or crumbled plant-based cheese

2 Tbsp extra-virgin olive oil

1 Tbsp red wine vinegar

½ tsp kosher salt

GYROS

12 oz [340 g] Impossible Burger

4 tsp gyro seasoning, homemade (see note) or purchased

4 pita breads

To make the tzatziki, add all of the ingredients to a small bowl and stir to blend. Cover and refrigerate until ready to serve or up to 3 days.

To make the Greek salad, in a medium bowl, combine the tomatoes, cucumber, pepperoncini, onion, olives, and feta. In a small bowl, whisk together the olive oil, vinegar, and salt. Pour the oil mixture over the salad and toss gently to coat. Set aside at room temperature.

Preheat a grill for direct cooking over high heat (450°F/230°C). Brush the grill grates clean. Divide the Impossible Burger into four equal portions and shape into oval patties ¼ in [6 mm] thick. Season each side of the patties with ½ tsp gyro seasoning.

Grill the Impossible Burger until browned and cooked through, turning once, 1½ to 2 minutes per side. Using a metal spatula, transfer to a plate. Grill the pita breads just long enough to warm through, turning once, about 30 seconds. Transfer the pita breads to individual plates.

To assemble, top each pita bread with one-fourth of the salad. Place a patty on top of each salad, then top with some of the tzatziki. Fold the pitas over and serve at once, with the remaining tzatziki alongside.

Gyro Seasoning: *In a small bowl, whisk together ¾ tsp each dried oregano, dried marjoram, dried thyme, garlic powder, and 1 tsp kosher salt.*

MAKES 4 SERVINGS

QUESADILLAS WITH ROASTED CORN SALSA

CHEF J MICHAEL MELTON

The filling for these quesadillas is a quick solve for dinner, because you just mix everything together and throw it in a pan to brown, a technique that lets the onions, garlic, and cilantro keep a bit of their crunch and fresh flavor. It's a talented multitasker, too. You can make a batch, keep it in the fridge, and rewarm it to use in tacos, burritos, or salads all week. The roasted-corn salsa, from our chef, J Michael Melton, adds a pop of color and spicy, smoky, caramelized action. His skillet-roasting method is fast and foolproof. If you like a little extra char, try roasting the corn on a gas or charcoal grill. Any melty or plant-based cheese will work here, or for a silky, creamy alternative, try J Michael's Plant-Based Whiz (page 89).

ROASTED CORN SALSA

1 Tbsp vegetable oil

2 ears fresh corn, shucked

½ cup [85 g] quartered cherry tomatoes

½ avocado, peeled, pitted, and diced

½ cup [20 g] chopped fresh cilantro

¼ red onion, finely chopped

1 small jalapeño chile, minced

Juice of 1 lime

1 tsp kosher salt

FILLING

12 oz [340 g] Impossible Burger

½ bunch cilantro, chopped

½ yellow onion, minced

3 cloves garlic, minced

1 tsp sweet paprika

½ tsp ground cumin

¼ tsp ground coriander

¼ tsp ancho chile powder

½ tsp dried oregano

½ tsp kosher salt

1 Tbsp vegetable oil

Four 10-in [25-cm] flour tortillas

16 oz [455 g] shredded Mexican-blend cheese or plant-based cheese

3 Tbsp unsalted butter or plant-based butter spread

To make the salsa, heat a large, heavy skillet over medium heat until hot. Add the oil, then add the ears of corn. Cook, turning occasionally, until charred on all sides and cooked through, about 12 minutes. Transfer to a cutting board and let cool. Working with one ear of corn at a time, stand the corn on one end and use a sharp knife to cut the kernels off the cob. Transfer to a medium bowl. Using a spoon, hold each cob over the bowl and scrape the sides of the cob to remove the corn milk. Add the tomatoes, avocado, cilantro, onion, jalapeño, lime, and salt to the pan and gently toss to combine. Set aside until ready to use, or cover and refrigerate for up to 12 hours before serving.

To make the filling, crumble the Impossible Burger into a large bowl. Add the cilantro, onion, garlic, paprika, cumin, coriander, chile powder, oregano, and salt and stir together until well combined.

In the skillet over medium heat, warm the oil. Add the Impossible Burger mixture and cook, stirring to break up the meat, until browned and cooked through, about 5 minutes. Remove from the heat and set aside.

To assemble the quesadillas, evenly cover half of a tortilla with ½ cup [2 oz/55 g] packed shredded cheese. Top with one-fourth of the meat mixture, spreading it into an even layer, then top with another ½ cup [2 oz/55 g] packed shredded cheese. Fold the other half of the tortilla over the filling. Repeat to form four quesadillas.

In the clean, large skillet over medium-low heat, melt 1 tsp butter. Add a quesadilla to the pan and cook until the cheese is melted and the tortilla is golden brown on the bottom, about 5 minutes. Add another 1 tsp butter to the pan and allow it to melt, then turn the quesadilla and cook until the second side is golden brown, 2 to 3 minutes. Transfer to a plate, cut into four wedges, and serve at once with the salsa. Repeat to cook all of the quesadillas.

MAKES 4 SERVINGS

TURKISH-SPICED SANDWICHES WITH GARLIC SAUCE

CHEF ERIK DROBEY

This plant-based version of the classic street food, döner kebap, is packed with flavorful spices, garlic, and pickles. "The trick to keeping the patties super juicy," says chef Erik Drobey of Wursthall in San Mateo, California, "is to start hot and to let the thin patties cook most of the time on the first side to really develop a well-browned crust. A quick flip and about 15 seconds on the second side ensures a nice pink center." Erik is partial to sesame and nigella seed–crusted Turkish-style bread. If you can't find it, he suggests sprinkling some of those seeds into the sandwich for a similar flavor effect. "During tomato season," he adds, "a big fat tomato slice or two elevates the entire sandwich to world-class status."

SPICED PATTIES

1½ lb [680 g] Impossible Burger

⅓ cup [15 g] chopped fresh oregano

3 cloves garlic, minced

1 Tbsp ground Aleppo pepper

1 Tbsp ground cumin

1 Tbsp ground sumac

1 Tbsp ground coriander

1½ tsp kosher salt

1½ tsp ground black pepper

GARLICKY WHITE SAUCE

15 cloves garlic, peeled

½ cup [120 g] mayonnaise or plant-based mayonnaise

1½ Tbsp tahini (sesame paste)

1½ tsp fresh lemon juice, or more to taste

Kosher salt

¼ cup [10 g] chopped fresh dill

3 Tbsp extra-virgin olive oil

SPICE BLEND

4 tsp ground Aleppo pepper

4 tsp ground cumin

4 tsp ground sumac

2 tsp kosher salt

ONION SALAD

1½ cups [165 g] thinly sliced red onion (about 1 red onion)

½ recipe Spice Blend (above)

3 cups [90 g] arugula leaves

1½ cups [45 g] cilantro leaves

6 crusty buns, such as Turkish or ciabatta rolls

Extra-virgin olive oil, for brushing

Dill pickle slices, for serving

1 ripe tomato, sliced (optional)

Flaky sea salt, for serving

1 Tbsp vegetable oil

Sliced pickled banana or cherry peppers, for serving

CONT. NEXT PAGE

To make the patties, line a large rimmed baking sheet with parchment paper. In a large bowl, combine the Impossible Burger, oregano, garlic, Aleppo pepper, cumin, sumac, coriander, salt, and black pepper and knead vigorously and thoroughly until the mixture is homogenous. Divide the mixture into six equal portions (4 oz/115 g each] and form into balls. Place the balls on the prepared baking sheet and press them into thin patties about ¼ in [6 mm] thick and slightly bigger than the diameter of the buns. Refrigerate while you make the sauce.

To make the sauce, fill a small saucepan half-full of water and add all but one of the garlic cloves. Bring to a boil over high heat, then drain and let cool for 5 minutes. Transfer to a food processor or blender. Add the mayonnaise, tahini, the ½ tsp lemon juice, the remaining garlic clove, and a big pinch of salt. Process until completely smooth, adding a little water if necessary to keep the sauce just thin enough to blend. Transfer to a medium bowl. Whisk in the dill and olive oil. Season to taste with salt and more lemon juice (if desired). Set aside.

To make the spice blend, in a medium bowl, whisk together all the ingredients. Transfer half of the mixture to a small bowl and set aside.

To make the onion salad, add the red onion to the spice blend in the medium bowl and toss until thoroughly coated. Add the arugula and cilantro, toss to combine, and set aside.

Brush the cut sides of the buns with olive oil and toast under a broiler, on a grill, or in a skillet until lightly charred and crisp. Spread the cut sides of each bun half with the garlic sauce, dividing it evenly. Portion the onion salad on top of each bottom bun. Drizzle with a little olive oil and season with a sprinkle of the reserved spice blend. Spread pickle slices on top of the red onion salad. Top with tomato slices (if using) and a sprinkle of flaky salt. Set aside.

In a well-seasoned cast-iron or nonstick skillet large enough to cook all of the patties at once, warm the vegetable oil over medium-high heat until shimmering. Carefully add the patties to the skillet and cook, without moving them for the first 30 seconds, until deeply browned with a crisp crust on the first side, about 2 minutes. Use a spatula to check and swirl the pan occasionally to make sure patties are not sticking. (Alternatively, cook the patties on a grill over direct high heat.)

Flip and continue to cook until the patties are medium-rare, 15 to 45 seconds longer. Immediately transfer the patties, browned side up, to the prepared buns. Top with the pickled peppers, sprinkle evenly with the remaining spice blend, add the bun top, and serve.

MAKES 6 SANDWICHES

CHEESESTEAKS WITH CARAMELIZED ONIONS

CHEF J MICHAEL MELTON

While experimenting with ways to create a plant-based cheesesteak with all the insanely mouth-watering appeal of the traditional version, Impossible Foods chef, J Michael Melton, came up with two game-changing hacks. First, there's the cheese. Non-dairy cheese can be plasticky when it melts. But melt it with an equal amount of water, and you get a plant-based "whiz" that keeps its silky texture, even at room temperature. Then, there are the caramelized onions. You don't actually brown these. Their deep, rich color and sweetness all comes from the reduced cola, and they cook up juicy and just right. The meat is simply crumbled and browned in a skillet. Put it all together, and you've found your new cheesesteak obsession.

COLA-CARAMELIZED ONIONS

2 large yellow onions, thinly sliced

One 20-oz [600-ml] bottle cola

PLANT-BASED WHIZ

7 oz [200 g] American-style plant-based cheese, cut into small cubes (about 1¾ cups)

¾ cup plus 3 Tbsp [210 ml] water

1 Tbsp vegetable oil

12 oz [340 g] Impossible Burger

Kosher salt and ground black pepper

Three 6-in [15-cm] hoagie rolls

½ cup [70 g] pickled hot peppers, sliced or chopped

To make the caramelized onions, line a large rimmed baking sheet with parchment paper. In a saucepan over medium-high heat, combine the onions and cola. Stir and bring to a simmer. Reduce the heat to medium-low to maintain a steady simmer and cook, stirring occasionally, until the cola is completely reduced and evaporated, about 1 hour. Make sure to watch the mixture so it doesn't burn. Remove from the heat and transfer the onions to the prepared baking sheet, spreading them into an even layer to cool. If not using right away, transfer to an airtight container and refrigerate for up to 5 days.

To make the plant-based whiz, add the cheese and water to a small saucepan. Bring to a simmer over medium heat, then whisk until smooth, about 2 minutes. Cover and set aside to keep warm until serving.

In a large nonstick skillet over high heat, warm the oil. Crumble the Impossible Burger into the pan and season with 1 tsp salt and a few turns of black pepper. Cook, stirring to break up the meat, until cooked through and the pieces start to form a brown crust, 3 to 4 minutes. Stir in the caramelized onions and warm through.

Divide the mixture among the hoagie rolls, then top with the plant-based whiz, dividing it evenly. Sprinkle with pickled hot peppers and serve at once.

MAKES 3 SANDWICHES

HERBED MEATBALLS WITH CHILE SAUCE AND YOGURT

LAURA KLIMAN

Impossible Foods Senior Flavor Scientist Laura Kliman is, naturally, obsessed with flavor. And when she entertains, she loves serving a spread of small plates with bold flavors, so people can enjoy lots of different tastes and textures. "These meatballs with yogurt and cucumbers give you a lot of bang for the bite," she says, "with layers of spicy, tangy, hot, and cool." For a totally plant-based version, you can use an egg substitute or omit the egg altogether.

CHILE SAUCE

2 pasilla chiles, seeded and chopped

1 tsp red pepper flakes

2 tsp ground cumin

3 Tbsp sherry vinegar

1 garlic clove, chopped

2 tsp smoked paprika

¼ tsp kosher salt

3 Tbsp olive oil

YOGURT SAUCE

½ cup [120 ml] plain whole-milk or plant-based yogurt

¼ cup [10 g] chopped fresh mint

Finely grated zest of 1 lemon

Kosher salt

HERBED MEATBALLS

½ small yellow onion, chopped

6 cloves garlic, chopped

¾ cup [30 g] chopped fresh cilantro

¾ cup [30 g] chopped fresh flat-leaf parsley

1 large egg, or 1 flax egg made from 1 Tbsp ground flaxseeds and 3 Tbsp water

¾ tsp ground cumin

1 tsp sweet paprika

¼ tsp ground coriander

1½ tsp kosher salt

12 oz [340 g] Impossible Burger

1½ tsp olive oil

½ cucumber, thinly sliced

Fresh mint leaves, for garnish

Red pepper flakes, for garnish

To make the chile sauce, in a small, dry skillet over medium heat, toast the chiles, pepper flakes, and cumin, tossing occasionally, until fragrant, about 3 minutes. Remove from the heat and let the mixture cool. Using a spice mill or mortar and pestle, grind to a fine powder.

Transfer the spice mixture to a food processor and add the vinegar, garlic, paprika, and salt. Process until smooth. With the motor running, gradually add the oil in a slow stream, processing until combined. Transfer to a large bowl and season to taste with salt. Set aside.

To make the yogurt sauce, in a small bowl, stir all the ingredients. Set aside.

To make the meatballs, clean the bowl of the food processor and pulse the onion, garlic, cilantro, and parsley until finely chopped. Transfer the onion mixture to another large bowl. Add the egg, cumin, paprika, coriander, and salt and stir to combine. Add the Impossible Burger and mix until everything is evenly combined. Using wet hands, scoop up 2 Tbsp of the mixture at a time and form into 1½-in [4-cm] balls. Place on a large rimmed baking sheet.

In a large skillet over medium heat, warm the oil. Working in batches, cook the meatballs, turning occasionally, until browned all over and cooked through, 5 to 7 minutes. Transfer the meatballs to the bowl with the chile sauce and gently toss to coat.

To assemble, spoon the yogurt sauce onto a serving platter and arrange the cucumber slices on top. Spoon the meatballs onto the yogurt mixture. Garnish with the mint leaves and a sprinkle of pepper flakes; serve.

MAKES 17 MEATBALLS; SERVES 4

SPICY COCONUT CURRY MEATBALLS

CHEF J MICHAEL MELTON

Feeling the need for some curry comfort food? You can sit down to a bowlful of these hearty meatballs in a rich, spicy-creamy curry sauce in less than an hour. "This recipe is a great choice for a dinner with friends, because you can make the sauce and bake the meatballs ahead of time, then rewarm the meatballs in the sauce on the day," says our chef, J Michael Melton. Serve them over white, jasmine, basmati, or brown rice, or make some noodles (spaghetti, rice noodles—whatever you've got on hand), toss them with the sauce, and spoon the meatballs over the top, Italian style. You can even add a sprinkling of toasted coconut for the Parm effect.

COCONUT CURRY

1 Tbsp vegetable oil

½ yellow onion, minced

2 Tbsp peeled and minced fresh ginger

2 cloves garlic, minced

2 tsp Madras curry powder

2 tsp ground coriander

½ tsp ground cumin

¼ tsp ground turmeric

¼ tsp ground Aleppo pepper

1 tsp kosher salt

2 Roma tomatoes, diced with their juices

3 Tbsp sambal oelek (chile paste)

One 13½-oz [400-ml] can coconut milk, well shaken

1 Tbsp brown sugar

MEATBALLS

12 oz [340 g] Impossible Burger

2 green onions, white and green parts, minced

2 cloves garlic, minced

2 Tbsp unsweetened coconut milk yogurt

1 Tbsp peeled and minced ginger

Juice of ½ lemon

¼ tsp ground coriander

¼ tsp ground cumin

¼ tsp Aleppo pepper

½ tsp kosher salt

Steamed rice, for serving

1 lime, cut into wedges

To make the curry sauce, in a large saucepan over medium heat, warm the oil. Add the onion, ginger, and garlic and cook, stirring, until the onion is translucent, about 2 minutes. Stir in the curry powder, coriander, cumin, turmeric, Aleppo pepper, and salt and cook, stirring, until fragrant, about 1 minute. Stir in the tomatoes and sambal oelek and cook, stirring, until the tomatoes have softened and started to break down, about 4 minutes. Add the coconut milk and sugar and bring to boil, stirring to combine. Reduce the heat to medium-low and simmer, stirring occasionally, until the sauce reduces slightly and the flavors have melded, about 30 minutes.

Meanwhile, make the meatballs. Preheat the oven to 425°F [220°C] and line a large rimmed baking sheet with parchment paper. Crumble the Impossible Burger into a large bowl. Add all the remaining meatball ingredients and mix together with your hands until well combined. Scoop 1 Tbsp of the mixture and form into 1½-in [4-cm] balls; you should have about 18 balls. Bake until browned and cooked through (145°F/63°C) on an instant-read thermometer), 7 to 9 minutes.

Transfer the meatballs to the warm sauce and simmer gently so the meatballs absorb the flavors, about 7 minutes. Serve the meatballs and sauce spooned over rice, with the lime wedges alongside.

MAKES 4 SERVINGS

TACOS DORADOS

CHEF TRACI DES JARDINS

"Tacos dorados, or fried rolled tacos, are a Mexican classic," says chef Traci Des Jardins, who served them by the dozens at her Mexican street-food inspired restaurant Mijita in San Francisco. "They're nothing like the taco-shell versions in American culture," she says, "but they do satisfy some of the nostalgia of those hamburger-based tacos with packaged seasoning mix so many Americans grew up eating. This recipe has a more authentic Mexican ring to it with the use of the complex guajillo chile and the kiss of a spicy and delicious tomatillo-avocado salsa."

8 oz [230 g] tomatillos, husked, rinsed, and quartered

1 serrano chile, stemmed and cut into thirds

½ bunch cilantro, 6 sprigs reserved for garnish, chopped

½ avocado, pitted and peeled

Kosher salt

4 guajillo chiles, halved, stemmed, and seeded

2 Tbsp vegetable oil

1 large yellow onion, finely chopped

4 cloves garlic, minced

12 oz [340 g] Impossible Burger

Sixteen 6-in [15-cm] corn tortillas

Vegetable oil, for frying

To make the salsa, add the tomatillos and serrano chile to a blender and blend until smooth. Add half of the chopped cilantro and blend until the cilantro is puréed and the mixture is bright green. Add the avocado and ½ tsp salt and blend until smooth. Taste and adjust the seasoning. Transfer to a serving bowl, or cover and refrigerate for up to 3 days.

Using kitchen shears, cut the guajillo chiles into fine strips. In a large, heavy skillet over medium-low heat, warm the oil. Add the onion and garlic and cook, stirring, until softened, about 8 minutes. Add the guajillo chile strips and cook, stirring, until softened, about 4 minutes. Transfer to a small bowl and set aside to cool; reserve the skillet.

Crumble the Impossible Burger into a large bowl and add 1 tsp salt, the cooled onion mixture, and the remaining chopped cilantro. Mix well to combine.

Preheat the oven to 200°F [100°C]. Clean and dry the reserved skillet and heat it over medium-low heat. Have ready a large baking sheet. One at a time, warm a tortilla on both sides, then spoon a scant 2 Tbsp filling slightly off center in an even line, leaving a ½-in [12-mm] border at either end of the line. Tightly roll the tortilla into a cylinder and fasten closed with a wooden toothpick at an angle through the center. Transfer to the baking sheet. Repeat to make 16 tacos.

Line a large baking sheet with paper towels. Add oil to a depth of 2 to 3 in [5 to 7.5 cm] to the same skillet. Warm the oil over medium-high heat until hot but not smoking, 325°F [165°C] on a deep-fry thermometer. Fry the tacos, in batches to avoid overcrowding, until crisp and golden brown, about 4 minutes. Using tongs, transfer to the prepared baking sheet and keep warm in the oven while frying the remaining tacos. Divide the tacos among individual plates, remove the toothpicks, and garnish each with a sprig of cilantro. Serve with the tomatillo salsa.

MAKES 16 TACOS; SERVES 6 TO 8

SZECHUAN MAPO TOFU

CHEF RICKY LEUNG

At the sleek, chic EMPRESS restaurant in Singapore, chef Ricky Leung is all about finding ways to use Impossible Burger meat in both classic and inventive takes on Chinese dishes. "I don't eat beef," he says, "but with Impossible Burger I can finally enjoy those classic dishes like mapo tofu that use a little beef for flavor and texture. It has a nice, firm bite that goes really well with the creamy softness of silken tofu." Szechuan peppercorns, the spice that gives mapo tofu an extra hit of lip-tingling heat, is worth tracking down. You can find it online or in Asian grocery stores. If it's not available, chef Ricky suggests adding a little more of the chili bean sauce to taste.

1 Tbsp vegetable oil

6 oz [170 g] Impossible Burger

1 Tbsp light soy sauce

¾ tsp dark soy sauce

½ tsp sugar

½ small carrot, peeled and diced

½ stalk celery, peeled and diced

3 green onions, green and white parts, finely chopped, plus 1 green onion, sliced, for garnish

1 Tbsp chili black bean sauce

2 Tbsp tapioca starch

One 16-oz [455-g] package silken tofu, cut into 1-in [2.5-cm] cubes

1 to 3 tsp Szechuan peppercorns, ground to a powder

1 tsp Szechuan peppercorn oil

Steamed white or brown rice, for serving

In a skillet over medium heat, warm the oil. Crumble the Impossible Burger into the pan and cook, stirring with a wooden spoon to break it up, until browned and fragrant, about 4 minutes. Remove from the heat.

In a large saucepan over high heat, stir together the soy sauces, sugar, and 2 cups [480 ml] water. Bring to a boil, then reduce the heat to medium and simmer until the sugar is dissolved, about 30 seconds. Add the carrot, celery, finely chopped green onions, and chili black bean sauce to the saucepan and cook, stirring, until the vegetables have softened, about 3 minutes.

In a small bowl, whisk together the tapioca starch and 2 Tbsp water until smooth, then whisk it into the simmering sauce. Add the Impossible Burger, tofu, peppercorn powder, and peppercorn oil. Cook, gently stirring, until fragrant, about 3 minutes. Garnish with the sliced green onion and serve at once with steamed rice.

MAKES 4 TO 6 SERVINGS

"I LOVE THAT LIGHTBULB MOMENT WHEN PEOPLE TRY THE IMPOSSIBLE BURGER AND THEY SMILE AND SAY, 'WOW … I COULD GET USED TO THIS!'"

Laura Kliman,
Senior Flavor Scientist,
Impossible Foods

KEFTEDES WITH LEMON AND MINT

CHEF MICHAEL SYMON

Keftedes are the go-to meatballs of Greece. And who better than chef Michael Symon to turn to for the definitive Impossible version? His classic recipe, perfectly seasoned and garnished with fresh mint and lemon zest, makes a nice light meal or finger-food appetizer. Serve keftedes straight up, or pair them with some Tzatziki (page 82), Greek Salad (page 82), or Israeli Salad (page 123) to round out the plate.

1 Tbsp vegetable oil, plus more for frying

1 small yellow onion, minced

Kosher salt

2 cloves garlic, minced

1 cup [60 g] diced good-quality white bread

1 cup [240 ml] whole milk or plant-based milk

1½ lb [680 g] Impossible Burger

2 large eggs, or 2 flax eggs made from 2 Tbsp ground flaxseeds and 6 Tbsp water

2 tsp oregano

½ tsp ground coriander

½ tsp ground cumin

¼ tsp ground cinnamon

⅛ tsp freshly grated nutmeg

Ground black pepper

½ cup [65 g] all-purpose flour

1 cup [40 g] torn fresh mint leaves

3 lemons

Extra-virgin olive oil, for drizzling

Coarse sea salt, for sprinkling

To make the keftedes, in a skillet over medium heat, warm 1 Tbsp oil. Add the onion and ½ tsp salt and cook, stirring, until the onion begins to soften, about 2 minutes. Add the garlic and cook, stirring, until softened, about 1 minute. Transfer to a large bowl and let cool completely.

In a bowl, toss together the bread and milk and let soak for about 2 minutes. Squeeze the bread, discarding the milk, and add the bread to the bowl with the onion mixture. Crumble the Impossible Burger into the bowl and add the eggs, oregano, coriander, cumin, cinnamon, nutmeg, ½ tsp salt, and 1 tsp black pepper. Mix the ingredients with your hands until evenly distributed.

Have ready a large baking sheet. Line another baking sheet with paper towels. Put the flour in a shallow bowl.

To form the meatballs, scoop 1 heaping Tbsp of the meatball mixture with wet hands and form into 1½-in [4-cm] balls. Roll each ball in the flour to evenly coat, shake off any excess, then transfer to the unlined baking sheet.

Fill a large skillet one-third full with oil. Warm the oil over medium heat until hot but not smoking, about 350°F [180°F] on a deep-fry thermometer. Fry the keftedes in two batches, turning once, until golden brown on the outside but still moist inside, about 5 minutes. Using a slotted spoon, transfer to the paper towel–lined baking sheet to drain.

To serve, arrange the keftedes on a platter. Grind some fresh pepper on top, then sprinkle with the mint leaves. Grate the zest of two of the lemons over the top, then finish with a drizzle of extra-virgin olive oil and a sprinkle of sea salt. Cut the lemons into wedges and arrange on the platter, then serve.

MAKES ABOUT 28 KEFTEDES; SERVES 4 TO 6

CHILES RELLENOS

CHEF TRACI DES JARDINS

Traditional chiles rellenos are battered and deep-fried, but Chef Traci Des Jardins favors this lighter (and easier) approach. She stuffs roasted poblanos or pasillas with a sweet-savory picadillo like the kind that's used in *chiles en nogada*, a beloved Mexican stuffed chile that's virtually unknown outside Mexico. "Without all that fried batter, you really taste the interplay of the chile and the filling," says Traci. "And this version is completely plant-based so it makes a great meatless entrée."

8 fresh poblano or pasilla chiles

PICADILLO

2 Roma tomatoes

3 Tbsp vegetable oil

1 yellow onion, finely diced

2 cloves garlic, minced

2 Tbsp raisins

12 oz [340 g] Impossible Burger

½ tsp dried oregano, preferably Mexican

¼ tsp ground cumin

Pinch of ground cinnamon, preferably Mexican

Pinch of ground allspice

Pinch of ground cloves

Leaves from 1 small bunch fresh flat-leaf parsley

¼ cup [30 g] slivered almonds, toasted

1 tsp sesame seeds, toasted

Kosher salt and ground black pepper

To roast the chilies, line a large rimmed baking sheet with paper towels. Using tongs, roast each chile over an open flame on the stove top, turning until blackened all over, 8 to 10 minutes. Alternatively, preheat the broiler, place the chiles on a baking sheet, and broil, turning as needed, until blackened on all sides. Transfer the chiles to a bowl and cover with plastic wrap or place in a zip-top plastic bag. Let steam for about 5 minutes to help loosen the skins. Rinse the chilies under water and remove the charred skin. Make a 2-in [5 cm] slit toward the middle of the chile. Using a teaspoon, carefully remove as many of the seeds and membrane as possible. Arrange the chiles on the prepared baking sheet. Set aside.

To make the picadillo, bring a saucepan half full of water to a boil over high heat. Add the tomatoes and blanch for 10 seconds. Using a slotted spoon, transfer to a bowl of ice water. When cool, peel and discard the skins. Cut each tomato in half crosswise, squeeze out the seeds, then chop into ¼ in [6 mm] dice. Set aside.

In a skillet over medium-high heat, warm 1 Tbsp oil. Crumble the Impossible Burger into the skillet and cook, stirring occasionally, until browned and cooked through, about 3 minutes. Add the oregano, cumin, cinnamon, allspice, and cloves and mix well, then season with salt and pepper. Transfer to a bowl and set aside.

Add the remaining oil to the skillet. Reduce the heat to medium-low and add the onion, garlic, and tomato. Cook, stirring, until the onions soften, about 10 minutes. Add the raisins and cook for 2 minutes. Add this mixture to the meat mixture and stir. Set aside 1 Tbsp parsley, 1 tsp almonds, and some sesame seeds for garnish. Add the remaining parsley, almonds, and sesame seeds to the meat mixture. Mix well.

To assemble, preheat the oven to 375°F [190°C]. Spoon the picadillo into each chile through the slit in the center, filling it as much as possible and dividing the picadillo between the chilies. Transfer the chilies to a large baking sheet. Roast until heated through, 15 to 20 minutes. Serve garnished with the remaining parsley, almonds, and sesame seeds.

MAKES 4 SERVINGS

LOMO SALTADO

CHEF TRACI DES JARDINS

One of Peru's best-loved dishes, lomo saltado is a stir-fry of steak and French fries. "It's an unexpected mix of cuisines, ingredients, and traditions that really works," says chef Traci Des Jardins. "You've got the influences of Chinese immigrants—stir-frying, soy sauce, rice—combined with Latin elements like potatoes, spices, and yellow chile paste. Unlike some 'fusion' dishes, this one is truly the best of both worlds, and with Impossible Burger meat you can make it meatless without compromising the flavor." For a shortcut, you can use frozen French fries. Just crisp them in the oven according to the package directions and add them to the mix just before serving.

½ recipe French fries (page 45), or 12 oz [340 g] frozen French fries

SPICED MEAT

3 Tbsp aji amarillo paste (Peruvian yellow chile paste)

4-in [10 cm] piece fresh ginger, peeled and grated

2 cloves garlic, minced

¼ tsp ground cumin

¼ cup [60 ml] soy sauce

¼ cup [60 ml] red wine vinegar

3 Tbsp vegetable oil

12 oz [340 g] Impossible Burger

½ red onion, halved lengthwise and julienned

2 Roma tomatoes, each cut into 8 wedges

4 green onions, white and green parts, finely sliced on the diagonal

¼ cup [60 ml] vegetable stock

Kosher salt

Ground pepper

½ cup [20 g] fresh cilantro leaves

1½ cups [300 g] steamed rice, warmed

If making homemade fries, cook the French fries for the first round of frying, according to the recipe directions. Set aside while you make the spiced meat.

To make the spiced meat, in a bowl, stir together the aji amarillo paste, ginger, garlic, and cumin. In another bowl stir together the soy sauce and vinegar. Set aside.

In a large skillet over medium-high heat, warm the oil. Crumble the Impossible Burger into the skillet and cook, without stirring, until browned on one side, about 2 minutes. Using a spatula, turn the meat and cook the other side until browned, about 1 minute. Add the red onion and tomato and cook, stirring to break up the meat, until the red onions and tomatoes are slightly wilted, 1 to 2 minutes. Add the green onions and reserved aji amarillo mixture, and cook for 1 minute. Stir in the soy sauce mixture and vegetable stock, then season with salt and pepper. Cook, stirring occasionally, until everything is steamy and hot, about 1 minute longer. Remove from the heat and cover to keep warm.

To finish the fries, fry them a second time according to the recipe, drain on a paper towel–lined baking sheet, then transfer to a wide shallow bowl. Alternatively, cook the frozen fries according to package instructions, then transfer the hot fries to a wide shallow bowl.

Add the spiced meat mixture to the fries, along with half of the cilantro leaves. Toss together well. Spread the rice onto a serving platter in an even layer, and top with the lomo saltado. Garnish with the remaining cilantro and serve at once.

MAKES 4 SERVINGS

TAGLIATELLE WITH BOLOGNESE SAUCE

CHEF MICHAEL SYMON

Chef Michael Symon's classic Bolognese sauce is perfect for tossing with tagliatelle, spaghetti, rigatoni, or just about any pasta. It will hold its own in a lasagna or risotto, too. For a restaurant-level experience, try it with fresh tagliatelle. You'll need about 1½ lb [680 g] fresh noodles to equal the same amount as 1 lb [455 g] dried pasta.

2½ Tbsp extra-virgin olive oil, plus more if needed

12 oz [340 g] Impossible Burger

Kosher salt

1 carrot, peeled and coarsely chopped

1 stalk celery, coarsely chopped

1 small yellow onion, coarsely chopped

2 cloves garlic, minced

1 cup [240 ml] dry red wine

One 15-oz [430-g] can whole San Marzano tomatoes, chopped, with juices

3 sprigs fresh oregano

1 fresh bay leaf

Pinch of red pepper flakes

1 lb [455 g] dried tagliatelle pasta

½ cup [20 g] chopped fresh flat-leaf parsley, plus more for garnish

¼ cup [30 g] grated Parmesan cheese or plant-based cheese, plus more for garnish

1 Tbsp unsalted butter or plant-based butter spread, plus more if needed

In a large Dutch oven over medium-high heat, warm 1½ Tbsp of the oil. Crumble the Impossible Burger into the pot and add a big pinch of salt. Cook, stirring to break up the meat, until browned, about 4 minutes. Meanwhile, in a food processor, pulse the carrot, celery, and onion to chop finely.

Using a slotted spoon, transfer the browned Impossible Burger to a bowl. Add the carrot mixture to the pot with a big pinch of salt and cook, stirring, until translucent and aromatic, 3 to 4 minutes. Add the garlic and cook, stirring, until fragrant, about 1 minute.

Add the red wine and stir to scrape up any browned bits from the bottom of the pan. Bring the mixture to a simmer, then lower the heat to medium and cook, stirring occasionally, until the liquid is reduced by about half, 3 to 5 minutes. Add the tomatoes, oregano, bay leaf, pepper flakes, and another big pinch of salt. Stir to combine, then simmer until thickened and fragrant, about 10 minutes. Add the Impossible Burger to the pot and simmer, stirring occasionally, until the flavors of the sauce have deepened, 20 to 30 minutes longer. Season to taste with salt.

While the sauce is simmering, bring a large pot of salted water to a boil. About 10 minutes before the sauce is ready, add the pasta to the boiling water, stir, and cook until al dente, about 7 minutes or according to the package instructions. Reserve ½ cup [120 ml] pasta water, then drain the pasta in a fine-mesh sieve.

Remove the herbs from the sauce, then add the pasta and stir to coat the noodles completely. Add 2 Tbsp of the reserved pasta water, the ½ cup [20 g] parsley, the ¼ cup [30 g] Parmesan, the 1 Tbsp butter, and the remaining 1 Tbsp oil and stir until the mixture is well combined and the butter is melted, adding more pasta water, butter, and oil if desired. Divide among individual plates or shallow bowls, garnish with parsley and Parmesan, and serve at once.

MAKES 4 TO 6 SERVINGS

VIETNAMESE MEATBALLS WITH NUOC CHAM

CHEF QUE VINH DANG

Get ready to fall in love with this classic Vietnamese combo of sweet, sour, savory, and herbaceous flavors. These authentic meatballs are an easy way to enjoy them at home any time. "These were one of my favorite things to eat growing up," says Vietnamese-born, Hong Kong-based chef Que Vinh Dang. "Normally, of course, they're made with meat, but the Impossible Burger fits seamlessly as a substitute without losing any of the eating enjoyment, and you can serve them in a variety of ways." They're great with steamed rice or over room-temperature rice noodles, chopped lettuce, or lettuce cups, and they're also great in a banh mi sandwich. To serve them as a party snack, skewer them on bamboo picks and arrange them on a platter with some shredded lettuce to keep them from rolling around, with a bowl of the nuoc cham for dipping.

NUOC CHAM

1 red or green Thai chile, finely chopped (seeds removed if less heat is desired)

Juice of 1 lime

1 Tbsp vegetarian fish sauce or coconut aminos

1 Tbsp soy sauce

1 Tbsp sugar

½ clove garlic, minced

MEATBALLS

12 oz [340 g] Impossible Burger

1 cup [40 g] fresh cilantro leaves

2 medium shallots, minced

2 Tbsp peeled and minced fresh ginger

2 Tbsp minced lemongrass

1 Tbsp vegetarian fish sauce or coconut aminos

1 Tbsp soy sauce

1 Tbsp sugar

1½ cloves garlic, minced

Ground black pepper

Steamed rice, cooked rice noodles, or lettuce cups for serving

To make the nuoc cham, in a bowl, whisk together the chile, lime juice, fish sauce, soy sauce, sugar, garlic, and ¼ cup [60 ml] water. Set aside.

To make the meatballs, finely chop half of the cilantro leaves (set aside the remaining leaves for garnish). Crumble the Impossible Burger into a bowl and add the chopped cilantro, shallot, ginger, lemongrass, fish sauce, soy sauce, sugar, garlic, and a few grinds of pepper. Stir to combine well. Scoop up about 1½ Tbsp of the mixture and form into 1¾ in [4.5 cm] balls. Transfer to a baking sheet; you should have 16 to 18 meatballs total.

To cook the meatballs, preheat a grill for direct cooking over medium-high heat, (425°F/215°C), or preheat a stove-top grill pan over medium-high heat. Brush the grill grates or grill pan clean, then brush with oil. Grill the meatballs, turning occasionally to brown all sides, until cooked through, about 6 minutes.

To serve, top the rice, noodles, or lettuce cups with meatballs. Garnish each serving with cilantro leaves and drizzle with some of the nuoc cham. Serve with additional nuoc cham alongside.

MAKES 4 SERVINGS

BAKED ZITI WITH BROCCOLI RAGÙ

CHEFS KEN ORINGER AND JAMIE BISSONNETTE

Baked pasta dishes are just the thing for feeding a group of friends, because you can do all the work ahead of time and then relax with the crowd while your oven finishes the job. Broccoli and sausage are a classic Italian combo, and this easy baked ziti from Boston-based chefs Ken Oringer and Jamie Bissonnette starts with Impossible Burger meat seasoned to taste like Italian sausage, and then gets a major infusion of finely chopped broccoli for extra flavor and vegetable goodness. The sauce is also perfect for tossing with pasta, like orecchiette, shells, or cavatappi.

FENNEL SAUSAGE

½ tsp fennel seeds

½ tsp coriander seeds

1½ lb [680 g] Impossible Burger

3 cloves garlic, minced

1 tsp smoked paprika

½ tsp red pepper flakes

1 tsp kosher salt

1½ tsp ground black pepper

16 oz [455 g] ziti pasta

Kosher salt

2 Tbsp olive oil

½ yellow onion, diced

2 cloves garlic, minced

1 lb [455 g] broccoli, stemmed and finely chopped

½ cup [120 ml] dry white wine

One 28-oz [800-g] can crushed tomatoes

2 cups [480 ml] vegetable broth

8 oz [230 g] whole-milk ricotta or plant-based ricotta (1 cup)

16 oz [455 g] mozzarella or plant-based mozzarella, shredded

½ cup [55 g] grated pecorino romano or Parmesan or plant-based Parmesan

To make the sausage, in a small skillet over medium-low heat, toast the fennel and coriander seeds, shaking the pan occasionally, until darkened and fragrant, about 8 minutes. Grind to a powder in a spice grinder or with a mortar and pestle, then add to a large bowl. Crumble the Impossible Burger into the bowl and add the garlic, paprika, pepper flakes, salt, and black pepper. Mix together with your hand until combined, then set aside for 10 minutes for the ingredients to bloom.

Preheat the oven to 375°F [190°C]. To a large pot of boiling water, add 2 Tbsp salt and then the pasta. Cook, stirring once or twice, until the pasta is al dente, 6 to 8 minutes, or according to package instructions. Drain and run under cool water to stop the cooking. Set aside.

In a large pot over medium heat, brown the sausage mixture, stirring to break up the meat, until cooked through, about 5 minutes. Transfer the sausage mixture to a bowl and set aside.

To finish the ragù, in the same pot, warm the oil over medium heat and add the onion and garlic. Cook, stirring, until tender, about 3 minutes. Add the broccoli and cook, stirring, until the color of the broccoli dulls, 8 to 10 minutes. Stir in 2 Tbsp water as needed. Add the wine and cook, stirring, until it evaporates, about 1 minute. Add the sausage mixture and cook, until well mixed, about 3 minutes. Add the tomatoes, broth, and 1 tsp salt, then bring to a simmer and cook, stirring, until slightly reduced, about 6 minutes. Adjust the seasoning.

To assemble, in a 9 by 13 in [23 by 33 cm] baking dish, layer 2 cups [480 ml] ragù, then half the pasta, then half the ricotta. Repeat the layers. Top with the remaining ragù, the mozzarella, and the pecorino. Bake until the sauce is bubbling and the cheese is golden brown, 25 to 30 minutes. Let stand 15 minutes, then serve.

MAKES 8 SERVINGS

SHEPHERD'S PIE WITH MASHED CELERY ROOT POTATOES

CHEF J MICHAEL MELTON

No shepherds were involved in the making of this recipe, but you'll find it every bit as satisfying as the animal-based original. Our chef, J Michael Melton, gives it a tasty twist by adding celery root to the mashed potato topping. "It's worth taking the time to chop the onion, carrot, and celery extra fine," he says. "You'll get a fully composed bite every time."

TOPPING

1½ lb [680 g] Yukon Gold potatoes, peeled and cut into ½-in [12-mm] chunks

1 lb [455 g] celery root, peeled and cut into ½-in [12-mm] chunks

Kosher salt and ground black pepper

¾ cup [180 ml] heavy cream or vegetable broth

4 Tbsp [55 g] unsalted butter or plant-based butter spread

3 Tbsp prepared horseradish

FILLING

1 Tbsp vegetable oil

1 yellow onion, finely chopped

1 carrot, peeled and finely diced

1 stalk celery, finely chopped

2 cups [340 g] fresh corn kernels

3 cloves garlic, minced

Kosher salt

1 cup [140 g] cremini mushrooms, finely chopped

1½ lb [680 g] Impossible Burger

2 Tbsp tomato paste

3 Tbsp finely chopped fresh thyme

Ground black pepper

1 cup [155 g] frozen petite peas

2 Tbsp dry red wine

To make the topping, add the potatoes and celery root to a large pot and fill with cold water to cover. Add 2 tsp salt, then bring to a boil over high heat. Reduce the heat and simmer until very tender, 15 to 20 minutes.

Meanwhile, make the filling. In a large skillet over medium-high heat, warm the oil. Add the onion, carrot, celery, corn, garlic, and 1 tsp salt and cook, stirring, until the onion is translucent, about 4 minutes. Add the mushrooms and cook, stirring, until they release their liquid and start to brown, about 2 minutes.

Crumble the Impossible Burger into the skillet and cook, stirring to break up the meat, until browned, about 4 minutes. Stir in the tomato paste until well combined, then add the thyme and a few turns of black pepper.

Add the red wine, stirring to scrape up any browned bits from the pan. Stir in the peas and cook until heated through, about 1 minute. Remove from the heat and cover to keep warm.

Preheat the oven to 400°F [200°F].

To finish the topping, drain the cooked potatoes and celery root in a fine-mesh sieve and transfer to a food processor. Add the cream, butter, horseradish, ¾ tsp salt, and a few turns of black pepper and process to a silky purée. Taste and adjust the seasoning.

Transfer the filling to a 9 by 13 in [23 by 33 cm] baking dish, spreading it evenly. Dollop with the mashed potato mixture, then spread it into an even layer, making swoops and ridges with a rubber spatula—the pointy bits will brown and crisp in the oven. Bake until the filling is bubbling and the top is golden brown, about 20 minutes. Transfer to a wire rack to cool slightly, about 15 minutes, then serve.

MAKES 6 TO 8 SERVINGS

CHAPTER 3
BURGERS

IMPOSSIBLE JARDINIÈRE BURGERS

CHEF TRACI DES JARDINS

If you're looking for a first-time recipe to showcase Impossible Burger meat in all its juicy, mouth-watering glory, this is a good place to start. After all, chef Traci Des Jardins gave the Impossible Burger its West Coast debut at her San Francisco restaurant Jardinière. "The expectations were high. People had been waiting with huge anticipation to try it," she remembers. "But the response was even better than we expected. Before long, we had regulars coming in more than twice a week to enjoy it."

2 Tbsp extra-virgin olive oil

3 yellow onions, thinly sliced

½ cup [120 ml] mayonnaise, preferably plant-based

3 Tbsp Dijon mustard

2 avocados, pitted and peeled

Kosher salt

1½ lb [680 g] Impossible Burger

Ground black pepper

6 oz [170 g] Gruyère or plant-based cheese, sliced (optional)

6 soft hamburger buns, split

4 Tbsp [55 g] unsalted butter or plant-based butter spread, at room temperature

6 romaine or Little Gem lettuce leaves, torn into bun-sized pieces

16 cornichons, thinly sliced lengthwise

In a heavy medium skillet over low heat, warm the oil. Add the onions and cook, stirring occasionally, until they are completely soft and slightly caramelized, about 50 minutes. Cover the skillet for the first half of cooking to allow the onions to soften, then remove the cover for the rest of the cooking time. Set aside.

Meanwhile, in a small bowl, stir together the mayonnaise and mustard. In another small bowl, mash the avocados with a pinch of salt. Divide the Impossible Burger into 6 equal portions (4 oz/115 g each) and form into patties ½ in [12 mm] thick.

Preheat a grill for direct cooking over high heat (450°F/230°C), or preheat a stove-top grill pan over medium-high heat. If using a grill, brush the grates clean.

Season both sides of the patties with a generous sprinkling of kosher salt and black pepper. Cook the burgers over direct heat or in the pan until grill-marked on the bottom, about 3 minutes. Turn the burgers, layer the cheese slices on the upturned cooked sides, and cook another 1½ minutes for medium-rare or 2 minutes for medium. Transfer the patties to a platter or cutting board.

Spread the cut sides of the buns with the butter and toast on the grill or in the grill pan until golden brown, about 30 seconds. Transfer the toasted buns to a platter or cutting board.

To assemble, spread the toasted sides of each bun with some of the Dijon mixture. Spread the top bun with some of the mashed avocado. Layer the bottom bun with sliced cornichons, a couple of pieces of lettuce, a patty, and then a large spoonful of caramelized onions. Top with the top bun and serve at once.

MAKES 6 BURGERS

IMPOSSIBLE BURGERS WITH POBLANO SALSA

CHEF BRAD FARMERIE

Sometimes, chef Brad Farmerie likes to keep things simple. Like with this plant-based burger he serves at Saxon + Parole in New York. "It's got just what it needs and nothing more," he says. "The paprika mayo adds a little smokiness that brings out the grilled flavor of the burger. And the heat, acidity, and texture of the salsa balance the richness of the Impossible Burger meat and the avocado." You can whip up the salsa and mayo ahead of time and keep them in the fridge for several days. Both go beautifully with charred broccoli or just about anything grilled.

POBLANO SALSA

3 poblano chiles, stemmed, seeded, and halved

½ tsp vegetable oil

½ small red onion, finely chopped

3 Tbsp extra-virgin olive oil

3 Tbsp lime juice (about 1 lime)

3 Tbsp green Tabasco sauce

1 tsp kosher salt

PAPRIKA MAYO

1 cup [240 ml] mayonnaise, preferably plant-based

1 Tbsp smoked paprika

1½ lb [680 g] Impossible Burger

Kosher salt and ground black pepper

6 seeded burger buns, split and toasted

1½ avocados, peeled, pitted, and thinly sliced

6 tomato slices (1 large beefsteak tomato)

6 red onion slices

6 butter lettuce leaves

To make the poblano salsa, preheat the oven to 450°F [230°C]. Line a baking sheet with aluminum foil and arrange the poblano halves skin side up on the baking sheet. Brush the chiles with the oil and roast until the skins are charred and the flesh is soft, about 15 minutes.

Transfer the chiles to a blender with the chopped red onion, olive oil, lime juice, Tabasco sauce, and salt. Blend to a chunky salsa. Taste and adjust the seasoning; set aside.

To make the paprika mayo, in a small bowl, whisk together the mayonnaise and paprika until well combined. Set aside.

Divide the Impossible Burger into 6 equal portions (4 oz/115 g each) and form into patties about ½ in (12 mm) thick. Season both sides with an even sprinkling of salt and pepper.

Preheat a grill for direct cooking over high heat (450°F/230°C), or preheat a stove-top grill pan over medium-high heat. If using a grill, brush the grates clean. Cook the burgers over direct heat or in the pan until well grill-marked on the bottom, about 4 minutes. Turn the burgers and cook about 2 minutes longer for medium-rare or about 4 minutes longer for medium. Transfer to a platter or cutting board.

While the patties cook, toast the cut sides of the burger buns over low heat on the grill or in the grill pan, about 5 minutes.

To assemble, spread 1 heaping Tbsp paprika mayo on the toasted sides of the buns. Top the bottom bun with a patty, then layer with 2 Tbsp poblano salsa, ¼ avocado, 1 tomato slice, 1 onion slice, and 1 lettuce leaf. Cap the burger with the top bun and serve at once. Alternatively, serve the burger with the onion, tomato, and lettuce on the side for diners to build their own burger.

MAKES 6 BURGERS

IMPOSSIBLE PARMESAN BURGERS

CHEF CHRIS COSENTINO

Chris Cosentino, chef-owner of Cockscomb in San Francisco, was one of the first chefs ever to serve Impossible Burgers. One of his variations gives the Impossible Burger the *alla parmigiana* treatment, dressing it with house-made marinara, fresh basil, a tangle of arugula, and a lacy golden Parmesan wafer—or *frico*—that adds a layer of umami and crunch. The wafer is a cinch to make (hey, it's got only one ingredient), and it's also a great way to add a little "wow" to salads and sandwiches. If you want to go totally plant-based, skip the Parmesan wafer and use potato chips or plant-based cheese crisps instead.

MARINARA SAUCE

3 Tbsp extra-virgin olive oil

½ red onion, finely diced

1 clove garlic, minced

1 bay leaf

3 fresh basil stems (optional)

3 fresh oregano stems (optional)

½ cup [120 ml] dry white wine

One 14½-oz [455-g] can San Marzano tomato purée

Kosher salt ground black pepper

FRICO

4 oz [155 g] Parmesan cheese, very thinly sliced

1½ lb [680 g] Impossible Burger

Kosher salt and ground black pepper

4 sesame burger buns, split

2 Tbsp extra-virgin olive oil

2 Roma tomatoes, cut into 12 thin slices

12 fresh basil leaves

1 cup [30 g] arugula

To make the marinara, in a sauté pan over medium-low heat, warm the olive oil. Add the onion, garlic, bay leaf, and herb stems (if using). Cook, stirring, until the onion is softened but not browned, about 6 minutes. Add the white wine and cook until completely reduced, about 8 minutes. Add the tomato purée and 1 tsp salt and cook until reduced by about half, about 40 minutes. Season to taste with salt and pepper. Cover to keep warm and set aside.

To make the Parmesan wafer, line a large baking sheet with parchment paper. In a medium nonstick skillet, arrange a thin layer of the cheese slices into a round 4 to 5 in [10 to 12 cm] in diameter. Cook over medium-low heat until the cheese has melted and turned a light golden brown, 10 to 15 minutes. Immediately use a thin metal spatula to transfer the wafer to the prepared baking sheet. Repeat to use the remaining cheese; you should have 4 wafers.

Form the Impossible Burger into four patties a little larger than the buns. Season both sides with a sprinkling of salt and pepper. Heat a large, heavy skillet over medium heat, add the patties, and cook, turning once, until browned on the outside and medium-rare inside, 4 to 6 minutes.

Brush the cut sides of the buns with the olive oil, then toast cut side down on a griddle or in a clean skillet over medium heat.

To assemble, layer the tomato slices on the bottom half of each bun, dividing evenly. Season the tomatoes with salt and pepper, then top each burger with three basil leaves. Add a burger patty to each portion, then top each patty with ¼ cup [60 ml] marinara. Top with one-fourth of the arugula, a Parmesan wafer, and the top bun. Serve at once.

MAKES 4 SERVINGS

IMPOSSIBLE JALAPEÑO BURGERS

CHEF PINKY COLE

"People hear vegan and they think fresh, healthy and . . . boring!" says Pinky Cole, founder of Atlanta's wildly popular plant-based burger spot, Slutty Vegan. "But sometimes even us vegans need to get a little naughty and feed our fast-food burger cravings. When I discovered the Impossible Burger, I knew I was ready to give the world lick-your-lips, juicy burgers that vegans could love—and everyone else could, too. For this one, we start by seasoning Impossible Burger meat with onions, garlic, cumin and coriander. Once the burger is cooked, we dress it up with plant-based toppings, like chipotle mayo and jalapeño cheese. It's spicy, juicy and, yeah, just the right amount of slutty."

1½ lb [680 g] Impossible Burger

½ cup [70 g] loosely packed, finely chopped yellow onion

¼ cup [20 g] finely chopped fresh flat-leaf parsley

4 cloves garlic, minced

2 tsp ground cumin

2 tsp ground coriander

2 tsp kosher salt

2 Tbsp vegetable oil

6 potato buns, split

6 Tbsp [85 g] chipotle mayonnaise, preferably plant-based

6 oz [170 g] pepper jack cheese, preferably plant-based, sliced (optional)

6 tomato slices (about 1 large beefsteak tomato)

6 Tbsp sliced pickled jalapeños

1½ cups [115 g] shredded iceberg lettuce

In a large bowl, combine the Impossible Burger, onion, parsley, garlic, cumin, coriander, and salt and mix until well combined.

Divide the Impossible Burger into six equal portions (4 oz/115 g each) and form into patties ½ in [12 mm] thick. Heat a large, heavy skillet over medium heat, then add the oil. Add the patties, in batches if necessary, and cook, turning once, until browned on the outside and medium-rare inside, about 6 minutes.

Toast the cut sides of the burger buns over low heat on a lightly-oiled griddle or skillet, about 2 minutes.

To assemble, spread the toasted sides of each bun with some of the chipotle mayonnaise. For each burger, top the bottom bun with a patty, then layer 1 oz sliced cheese, 1 tomato slice, 1 Tbsp pickled jalapeño, and some lettuce on top, dividing it evenly. Cap the burger with the top bun and serve at once.

MAKES 6 BURGERS

SLIDERS WITH ISRAELI SALAD AND HUMMUS

CHEF JUSTIN CUCCI

"Don't get me wrong, I love a good burger," says chef Justin Cucci, "but to me, sliders hit the sweet spot with just the right proportions of everything in a few perfect bites." These sliders from his menu at Linger in Denver, Colorado, get that balance just right. The Montreal steak seasoning is essentially a pastrami spice mix. Justin notes that you can also go more Middle Eastern by swapping it with ras el hanout or za'atar. His slider bun of choice is a Hawaiian roll. "You want something mild-tasting, and it's got to be really soft," he says, "so all the ingredients don't get squeezed out when you take that first bite."

HUMMUS

One 15-oz [445-g] can chickpeas, drained and rinsed

¾ cup [190 g] tahini

½ cup [120 ml] fresh lemon juice

1½ tsp ground cumin

1 tsp kosher salt

2 tsp extra-virgin olive oil

2 tsp grapeseed oil

ISRAELI SALAD

1 Tbsp sherry vinegar

1 Tbsp minced shallot

¾ tsp sugar

¼ tsp stone-ground Dijon mustard

Kosher salt and ground black pepper

1 Tbsp extra-virgin olive oil

1 Persian cucumber, thinly sliced

1 small tomato, diced

½ small red onion, thinly sliced

1 sprig fresh dill, coarsely chopped

1 sprig fresh mint, coarsely chopped

1½ lb [680 g] Impossible Burger

2 Tbsp Montreal steak seasoning

1 cup [115 g] shredded Havarti with dill

8 slider buns, split

1 avocado, peeled, pitted, and thinly sliced (optional)

½ Tbsp sesame oil

½ Tbsp black sesame seeds

To make the hummus, in a blender or food processor, combine the chickpeas, tahini, lemon juice, 3 Tbsp water, cumin, salt, and oils. Blend until smooth. Set aside ½ cup [120 ml] and save the rest for later; it will keep in an airtight container in the refrigerator for up to 1 week.

To make the salad, in a mason jar with a tight-fitting lid, add the vinegar, shallot, sugar, mustard, ¼ tsp salt, and some pepper. Seal and shake until homogenous. Slowly pour in the oil, seal, and shake vigorously until emulsified. Taste and adjust the seasoning.

In a medium bowl, toss together the cucumber, tomato, onion, dill, and mint with the vinaigrette.

Divide the Impossible Burger into eight equal pieces (3 oz/85 g each), then shape into patties ½ in [12 mm] thick. Season on both sides with the steak seasoning. In a large skillet over high heat, sear the patties on each side until a crust forms, about 1 minute per side. Top each patty with 2 Tbsp cheese. Cover the pan until the cheese melts, about 30 seconds.

Meanwhile, spread about 1 Tbsp hummus on each bottom bun. Divide the avocado slices among the cut sides of the top buns and use the tines of a fork to mash slightly onto the buns.

Transfer the patties to the bottom buns. Top each with 2 Tbsp salad. Place the bun tops on top. Lightly brush each bun top with sesame oil and sprinkle with black sesame seeds. Serve.

MAKES 8 SLIDERS; SERVES 4

PATTY MELTS WITH CARAMELIZED ONIONS

CHEF ANDREI SOEN

Chef Andrei Soen is a California native who lives and cooks in Singapore. "One of the things I missed most over here was a good sandwich," he says. So he decided to give Singapore its first world-class sandwich shop, and Park Bench Deli was born. "I wanted a burger on the menu," he says, "but it's a sandwich place, so I settled on a patty melt, because . . . well, I love patty melts. In Singapore, a lot of people don't eat beef. So, when the Impossible Burger came along, I gave it a try." His Impossible Burger melt is now selling in record numbers. "I could never take it off the menu," says Andrei. "Not that I'd ever want to."

CARAMELIZED ONIONS

3 Tbsp unsalted butter or plant-based butter spread

3 yellow onions, sliced

Kosher salt

SPECIAL SAUCE

¾ cup [180 ml] mayonnaise or plant-based mayonnaise

5 Tbsp [80 ml] ketchup

1½ Tbsp yellow mustard

1½ Tbsp finely chopped bread and butter pickles

1½ tsp Worcestershire sauce

1½ tsp white wine vinegar

¾ tsp sugar

¾ tsp kosher salt

PATTY MELTS

1½ lb [680 g] Impossible Burger

Kosher salt and ground black pepper

1 Tbsp vegetable oil, plus more if needed

12 slices American cheese or plant-based cheese

12 slices Jewish rye bread

1 cup [155 g] bread and butter pickle slices

3 Tbsp unsalted butter or plant-based butter spread

To make the onions, in a skillet over medium heat, melt the butter. Add a large handful of onions to the pan and cook, stirring, until softened, about 7 minutes. Repeat until you have added all the onions. Reduce the heat to low and cook, stirring occasionally, until the onions are richly brown, about 1 hour. If the pan gets dry, add a few Tbsp water; watch closely so they don't burn. Season with salt and set aside.

Meanwhile, make the special sauce. In a bowl, stir together all of the ingredients until combined. When the caramelized onions have cooled, finely chop 1 Tbsp and add it to the sauce. Cover and refrigerate until ready to use.

Divide the Impossible Burger into six equal pieces (4 oz/115 g each) and form into rectangular patties the size of the rye bread and ¼ in [6 mm] thick. Season with salt and pepper.

Preheat a cast-iron pan over high heat. Add the oil and when hot, add three patties. Cook until a crust forms, about 2 minutes, then flip. Add two slices cheese to each patty, then cook another 2 minutes. Transfer to a plate. Repeat with the remaining three patties, adding oil if needed.

To assemble the patty melts, spread one side of each slice of bread with the sauce, dividing it evenly. Layer six slices of bread with a patty, pickles, and caramelized onions, dividing evenly. Top each with a slice of bread, sauce side down.

Wipe out the pan. Melt half the butter over medium-high heat. Add three sandwiches in a single layer. Using a metal spatula, press the sandwiches down. Cook until golden brown and toasted on the bottom, about 3 minutes. Turn and toast the other side, about 1½ minutes longer. Repeat to cook the remaining sandwiches. Serve hot.

MAKES 6 PATTY MELTS

BARBECUE SLOPPY JOES

CHEF TANYA HOLLAND

Chef Tanya Holland's mom used to make sloppy Joes all the time when she was growing up. It was an easy one-pan meal, and she'd often serve a pickled-cucumber salad on the side. "It's such a distinctive, familiar combination of sweet, savory, and spice," Tanya says, "and with all that going on, it's a great choice to make with Impossible Burger meat." The green and red bell peppers are a nod to the Southern "trinity" of peppers, onions, and celery. She also throws in one of her best-loved seasoning secrets: a touch of brown sugar. "I'm such a fan, I even named my restaurant Brown Sugar Kitchen," she laughs.

2 Tbsp vegetable oil

1 small yellow onion, finely chopped

1 small green bell pepper, seeded and finely chopped

1 small red bell pepper, seeded and finely chopped

1 large stalk celery, finely chopped

Kosher salt

1½ lb [680 g] Impossible Burger

1¼ cups [300 ml] ketchup

2 Tbsp brown or grainy mustard

1 Tbsp firmly packed light brown sugar

1 Tbsp apple cider vinegar

1 tsp smoked paprika

1 tsp ground cumin

½ tsp ground black pepper

¼ tsp red pepper flakes

6 sesame or brioche burger buns, split

In a large, heavy skillet over medium heat, warm the oil. Add the onion, bell peppers, celery, and a large pinch of salt and cook, stirring occasionally, until the vegetables are softened and start to brown, about 7 minutes.

Crumble the Impossible Burger into the pan, then increase the heat to medium-high. Cook, stirring with a wooden spoon to break up the Impossible Burger, until browned, about 4 minutes. Add ½ cup [120 ml] water and stir to scrape up any browned bits from the bottom of the pan.

Add the ketchup, mustard, sugar, vinegar, paprika, cumin, 1 tsp salt, black pepper, and red pepper flakes, and bring to a simmer, stirring. Reduce the heat to low and simmer, stirring frequently, until the flavors come together and the mixture is slightly thickened, about 15 minutes. If the mixture becomes too thick, add a little water to thin it. Season to taste with salt and pepper, if necessary.

Toast the split sides of the buns. Top the bottom halves of the buns with the sloppy Joe mixture, dividing it equally. Cover with the bun tops and serve at once.

MAKES 6 SERVINGS

IMPOSSIBLE PAIRINGS

MADE POSSIBLE

This book is jam-packed with recipes and tips for enjoying the Impossible Burger. But what about pairing your creations with wine, beer, and other drinks?

It's simple. Just imagine you're looking for a match for a dish made with ground beef and go from there. Forget about that tired old rule "red wine with meat." Instead, think about the biggest flavors in the dish, and pair with them. You'll find that all kinds of drinks go with Impossible Burger dishes. Here are some basic tips, grouped by flavor families.

To add to the fun, we've also asked our friend Eric Wareheim to provide pairings for some of our recipes. Eric is the writer, director, producer, and actor known for such comedy hits as *Tim and Eric Awesome Show, Great Job!*, and *Master of None.* He's also an accomplished winemaker, and the co-owner of Las Jaras Wines.

ASIAN

In dishes like Asian Lettuce Wraps (page 46), Pan-fried Chive Pot Stickers (page 49), Vietnamese Phở (page 67), Xinjiang Pockets (page 56), and Southeast Asian Stuffed Flatbread (page 58), you get that mouthwatering balance of umami, salty, sweet, and heat. German and Austrian varietals like Reisling and Grüner Veltliner work well here. And of course, there's always the tried-and-true Asian beer route—when in doubt, go with a beer from the country of origin of your dish—as well as sake or a shochu cocktail.

Eric's pairing pick
Thai Laab with Fresh Herbs (page 64) with a 2015 Peter Lauer "Schonfels" Fass 11 Riesling GG.

"Spicy Thai food and bright electric German Reislings have been an obsession since I was introduced to the concept at Lotus of Siam in Las Vegas many moons ago. They have this great wine cellar and pushed this type of pairing versus the usual Singha beer thing. The spice in the Thai food, especially laab, came to life in an ethereal way. You're sweating but also floating in ecstasy as the finishes of both the wine and the bird's eye chilies dance around in your palate. Also, don't be afraid of an off-dry Riesling with your Thai (or other Asian) food. A slightly sweet wine can also take you to very special places."

LATIN

Milder Mexican and Latin-influenced dishes, like Picadillo Empanadas (page 39), Albondigas Soup (page 44), Taco Salad, (page 50) and Quesadillas with Roasted Corn Salsa (page 84) can totally pair with wine. Go for the crisp, fresh acidity of a Sauvignon Blanc, Albariño, or Pinot Grigio. Spicier, bolder dishes, like Tinga Tostadas with Pickled Cilantro Slaw (page 74) play well with Riesling or a red like Tempranillo or Zinfandel. Or go with a Margarita, a Paloma, or a Mezcal cocktail. A great Mexican craft beer is also a no-fail match. For a brunch dish, like Chilaquiles with Red Beans and Charred Tomatillo Salsa (page 77), try a Bloody Maria (made with tequila instead of vodka) or a Michelada.

Eric's pairing pick
Tacos Dorados (page 93) with a light red, such as 2018 Las Jaras Glou Glou.

"This wine made from our vineyards in Impossible Food's backyard, Mendocino County, is super easy to drink because each of the grape varieties in the blend is gently carbonically macerated to bring that fun pop and juiciness to each sip. I'd give it an hour or two in the fridge before pouring. You want that chilled freshness to cut down some of the spice on those tacos! You may think I'm biased for including TWO pairings from Las Jaras, but trust me, our wine is very similar in vibe and expression to the new exciting world of Impossible Burger goodness, and it just WORKS."

RED AND SAUCY

For bold, red-sauce Italian dishes, like Tagliatelle with Bolognese Sauce (page 103) or Baked Ziti with Broccoli Ragu (page 108), go with a full-bodied, jammy wine like Zinfandel or a robust Italian red like Sangiovese or Primitivo. When the weather starts to warm up, a big rosé or an ice-cold beer with some bitter notes would also be great choices.

Eric's pairing pick
Barbecue Sloppy Joes (page 127) with a bold red, such as 2018 Las Jaras Sweet Berry Wine.

"Sloppy Joes are all about extreme fun and extreme flavor. So is our sweet berry wine. To live the Sticky Sauce Life you gotta: a) get a bunch of BBQ buds together that don't mind getting their faces all messy with these Sloppy Joes; b) rinse it down with a slightly chilled juicy red; and c) hurry to get seconds and a top up 'cause both will be going FAST."

NEAR-EASTERN, AFRICAN, AND MEDITERRANEAN

It can be tricky to pair wine and other drinks with dishes from the Near East, Africa, and the Mediterranean that get their distinctive flavors from spices and herbs—dishes like Ethiopian-Spiced Meat with Hummus and Toasted Cashews (page 61), Herbed Meatballs with Chile Sauce and Yogurt (page 90), Turkish-Spiced Sandwiches with Garlic Sauce (page 87), Impossible Moroccan Cigars (page 34), and Gyros with Greek Salad, Tzatziki, and Grilled Pita (page 82). But that's the fun of it. Beer will make a good match with any of the above. Or you might go for the anise flavors of pastis, Pernod, or ouzo. A lighter, crisp, non-oaked white wine—like an herbaceous Sauvignon Blanc—can also work well.

CLASSIC BURGERS

For classic burgers, like the Impossible Jardinière Burgers (page 115), as well as sandwiches like Cheesesteaks with Caramelized Onions (page 89), go with a Malbec, Cabernet, Zinfandel, or a full-bodied Pinot Noir that has enough weight to bring out the meaty flavors of Impossible Burger as well as some acid to balance all those condiments like ketchup, mustard, pickles, and onions. And if you're not in the mood for wine, a great craft beer works every time.

Eric's pairing pick
Patty Melts with Caramelized Onions (page 124) with Asahi Super Dry Beer.

"I'm not a total wine-only guy, I swear! Sometimes you need a crisp, ice cold beer to hold up to a decadent Patty Melt. The greasier the better. The colder the better. I fell in love with this beer while traveling through Japan. They understand the concept of dry and COLD. Find yourself a nice chilled glass and you'll be in heaven."

CREATIVE BURGERS

Rule of thumb: The more you do to a burger, topping-wise, the more complex your wine should be. But complex doesn't have to mean pricey. Go for a red with a balance of fruit and acid with some tannins and heft to enhance the Impossible Burger's meaty notes. A not-too-huge Cabernet, Montepulciano d'Abruzzo, or Syrah/Shiraz would all be good choices.

Eric's pairing pick
Impossible Parmesan Burgers (page 118) with 2017 Podere le Boncie "Cinque" Rosso di Toscana.

"Due to the Italian vibe of this burger, I went with one of my favorite new Sangioveses from Tuscany. It's not your grandad's Chianti that's stuffy and huge and hard to take more than two sips. This beauty is gently macerated so it's more of a medium-bodied expression of the noble Sangiovese grape. Of course, it's fully organic with minimal additions to keep it clean and good for you."

That's our advice for pairing the Impossible Burger with good things to drink. But the best tip we can give you is to drink something you love that goes with all the other flavors you're surrounding it with. It's basically impossible to go wrong.

IT'S A GREAT TIME TO BE MEATLESS

I was vegetarian for seven years around the time I attended college at Temple University in Philadelphia. Those were trying times to be meatless. The dorms only offered pathetic grilled cheeses, and you know Philly is basically a cheesesteak paradise. NO veggie options. You'd be yelled at if you asked for anything but "Wiz Wit!" (which means Cheese Wiz and Onions on your Steak Sandwich). It was extremely hard to have yummy creative options back then.

But good Lord, times have changed! I've been experimenting with the Impossible Burger meat in my "SmashHeim" burger recipe and I'm fully, 100% sold. Even my most meaty of beef bros dig it. We often have BBQs or poker parties with Impossible Burgers paired with my Las Jaras wines.

—Eric Wareheim

CONTRIBUTORS

TRACI DES JARDINS

A California native of a small Central Valley agricultural community, Traci Des Jardins has been a part of the San Francisco food community for more than 22 years. During that time she has opened many great San Francisco restaurants, including her former flagship restaurant Jardinière, Public House, the Commissary, Arguello, and her newest addition, School Night. Traci has been a culinary advisor to Impossible Foods since 2015 and was one of the first chefs to launch the Impossible Burger in the summer of 2016. A dedicated philanthropist, Traci sat on the board of the local nonprofit La Cocina for many years and has been a longtime supporter of the farm-to-table movement and sustainability. Known as one of the top female chefs in the country, she is a two-time James Beard award-winner and has earned a number of industry accolades throughout her career.

J MICHAEL MELTON

J Michael Melton is the chef and head of culinary at Impossible Foods. He supports the Impossible Foods product and research development team from a culinary perspective and works with restaurant operators on menu innovation. He grew up in South Carolina, working in his uncle's restaurant and his parents' catering businesses. After completing a degree in business management, he earned an AA degree in culinary arts, cum laude, from Johnson & Wales University in Denver. From there, he went on to work in a number of prestigious kitchens in Colorado before moving back to South Carolina to become chef/partner of his own concept, Culina Modern Comfort Food. An offer to work with the Daniel Patterson Group as sous chef at Plum/Plum Bar/Ume brought him to California. J Michael joined Impossible Foods in 2017 and became head of culinary in 2019. He is proud to be part of a cutting-edge food/technology company that has the momentum to change the food world as we know it.

JAMIE BISSONNETTE

Jamie Bissonnette, a James Beard Award–winning chef, co-helms the Barcelona tapas restaurant Toro in Boston, NYC, and Dubai; Boston's beloved enoteca Coppa; and the global tapas restaurant Little Donkey in Cambridge, Massachusetts, and Bangkok. A champion of nose-to-tail cuisine, Jamie is the author of *The New Charcuterie Cookbook,* with a foreword by Andrew Zimmern.

MAY CHOW

Canadian-born Hong Kong chef May Chow, the genius behind Happy Paradise and Little Bao, was named Asia's Best Female Chef in 2017. Chow prides herself on reinventing Cantonese classics by showcasing underappreciated ingredients while remaining respectful of local traditions. Her culinary inventiveness and style create a compelling combination upon which she has built her international reputation. Chow has served as a guest judge for *MasterChef Asia, Top Chef* in America, and is a speaker at the Melbourne Food & Wine Festival.

PINKY COLE

Pinky Cole grew up in a single-parent family in Baltimore and graduated from Clark Atlanta University in 2009. After working as a television producer, she opened a juice bar and restaurant in New York. In 2018, she launched what would soon become one of Atlanta's most popular food trucks featuring plant-based fast-food. In 2019, she opened the brick-and-mortar Slutty Vegan location to bring the fresh, juicy indulgence of her signature plant-based burgers to Atlanta.

CHRIS COSENTINO

Chris Cosentino is co-owner of San Francisco's celebrated Cockscomb restaurant; Jackrabbit in Portland, Oregon; and Acacia House at Las Alcobas in Napa Valley. He is the author of *Beginnings: My Way to Start a Meal,* and *Offal Good: Cooking from the Heart, with Guts.* Cosentino won season four of Bravo's *Top Chef Masters* and is a member of Chefs Cycle, a 300–mile annual bicycle ride that raises funds and awareness in support of No Kid Hungry.

JUSTIN CUCCI

Justin Cucci is the founder of Denver's Edible Beats restaurant group, which includes Root Down, Root Down DIA, Linger, Ophelia's, Vital Root, and El Five. He is the author of *The Edible Beat* cookbook, has been featured in the *New York Times, Bon Appétit,* and *Condé Nast Traveler,* and has appeared on the Cooking Channel and the Travel Channel. Cucci's restaurants have won awards ranging from Design of the Year to Most Sustainable Menu. They are a diverse group with a common thread: vegetable-forward, sustainably sourced menus.

QUE VINH DANG

Born in Vietnam, Chef Que Vinh Dang grew up in New York, where he worked under such renowned chefs as Rocco DiSpirito and Geoffrey Zakarian. Since moving to Hong Kong, he has made a splash with everything from gourmet burgers to fine dining. His wildly popular TBLS featured refined Vietnamese comfort food. In 2014, he launched Hong Kong's first brew pub and opened a fine-dining restaurant, Quest by Que. His current venture, NHAU offers fresh, modern takes on Vietnamese flavors.

ERIK DROBEY

Erik is a sous chef at Wursthall Restaurant and Bierhaus in San Mateo, California, where he developed and launched Wursthall's housemade sausage program. Erik lives in San Francisco with his son and Kiki the cat who loves chasing foil balls but not eating Erik's cooking. Thankfully, Erik's son does enjoy eating what Erik cooks, including Impossible Burger meatballs with tomato sauce.

BRAD FARMERIE

Brad Farmerie's career started with seven years of experience in London's best kitchens. In 2003, he opened PUBLIC in New York, which garnered a Michelin star, and then Saxon + Parole in 2011, followed by its branches in Moscow and Auckland. He has developed Ghost Donkey, the Poni Room, JetBlue's business-class menu, and restaurants on the Virgin Voyages cruise line. He was named a StarChefs Rising Star and a Food Arts Emerging Tastemaker, and won Iron Chef America.

SUSAN FENIGER

Iconic culinarian and entrepreneur Susan Feniger is best known for her Border Grill and Socalo restaurants, which she runs with business partner, Mary Sue Milliken. Susan has co-authored six cookbooks, starred on the Food Network's popular *Too Hot Tamales* series and competed on Bravo's *Top Chef Masters*. In 2018, Feniger and Milliken were named the recipients of the Julia Child Award and honored with the LA Times' Gold Award.

TANYA HOLLAND

Known for her inventive take on modern soul food, Tanya Holland is the executive chef/owner of Brown Sugar Kitchen in Oakland and San Francisco, California. She is the author of *Brown Sugar Kitchen* and *New Soul Cooking,* was the host and soul food expert on the Food Network series *Melting Pot,* and competed on the fifteenth season of Bravo's *Top Chef.* She holds a degree in Russian Language and Literature from the University of Virginia and a Grand Diplôme from La Varenne Ècole de Cuisine.

DOUGLAS KEANE

Douglas Keane got interested in cooking as a young boy helping his mother in their Michigan kitchen. After graduating from Cornell University's School of Hotel Administration, he worked for a decade in some of the America's best kitchens, including the Four Seasons and Lespinasse in New York. In San Francisco, he was chef de cuisine at Jardinière. In 2004, he and partner Nick Peyton opened Cyrus, which garnered several local and national awards.

RICKY LEUNG

Chef Ricky Leung has more than 25 years of cooking experience at multiple award-winning restaurants. Through a combination of innovativeness and a deep understanding of Cantonese cuisine, he is able to retain the magic of traditional Chinese cooking while creating delicious dishes that are more relevant to today's world. He is Executive Head Chef at EMPRESS (part of The Privé Group), where his unique brand of creativity and cooking skills have led the restaurant to be featured in the 2018 Michelin Guide for Singapore.

MARY SUE MILLIKEN

Mary Sue Milliken is a James Beard and Julia Child Award–winning chef best known for her modern Mexican Border Grill restaurants in Los Angeles and Las Vegas, and the Food Network series *Too Hot Tamales*, both created with business partner Susan Feniger. Milliken is passionate about food policy and works with various nonprofits around the world to bring her expertise to help shape sustainable food systems.

KWAME ONWUACHI

Washington, DC–based Kwame Onwuachi is the chef of Kith and Kin, where he serves Afro-Caribbean cuisine influenced by his family ties to Louisiana, Jamaica, Trinidad, and Nigeria. In 2019, he published *Notes from a Young Black Chef,* the story of his childhood in New York and Nigeria and the opening of his first restaurant, Shaw Bijou. He won the James Beard Award for Rising Star Chef, was named one of *Food & Wine's* Best New Chefs, and has appeared on *Top Chef.*

KEN ORINGER

James Beard Award–winning chef Ken Oringer has built an empire of restaurants inspired by his global travels. They include the Tsukiji fish market–style Uni at the Eliot Hotel in Boston; the Roman enoteca Coppa in Boston's South End; the Barcelona tapas bar Toro in Boston, NYC, and Dubai; and Little Donkey in Bangkok and Cambridge, Massachusetts, whose menu is inspired by Ken's world travels.

TAL RONNEN

Tal Ronnen, founder and chef of Crossroads in Los Angeles and author of the New York Times bestseller, *The Conscious Cook,* became known nationwide as the chef for Oprah Winfrey's twenty-one-day cleanse. He made his culinary mark at a number of high-profile events, including Ellen DeGeneres and Portia de Rossi's wedding, Arianna Huffington's Democratic National Convention party, and a Senate dinner. Tal conducts master vegetarian workshops for students and staff at Le Cordon Bleu campuses nationwide.

SARAH SCHAFER

Owner and executive chef of Irving Street Kitchen, Sarah Schafer is one of Portland's powerhouse female chefs, always on the cutting edge of the local food scene with her casually elegant American cuisine. After graduating from the Culinary Institute of America in 1993, she worked under some of the most respected chefs in the restaurant industry, such as Daniel Patterson, Ken Oringer, and Tom Colicchio.

ANDREI SOEN

Singapore-born and San Francisco Bay Area–raised Andrei Soen is the brains behind Singapore's favorite sandwich shop, Park Bench Deli. The popular spot pays tribute to the great sandwiches of the world, with everything kept simple and old school—just as it should be, in its purest form and in all its glory.

MICHAEL SYMON

Growing up in a Greek and Sicilian family, Cleveland native Michael Symon creates boldly flavored, deeply satisfying dishes at his restaurants in America's heartland: Lola, Mabel's BBQ, Roast, Bar Symon, and B Spot Burgers. A former co-host on ABC's *The Chew,* he shares his exuberant, approachable cooking style and infectious laugh with viewers as an Iron Chef on the Food Network and the host of the Cooking Channel's *Burgers, Brew & 'Que.* Michael is the author of four best-selling cookbooks.

ERIC WAREHEIM

Eric Wareheim is a writer, director, producer, actor and winemaker, known for his groundbreaking comedic collaborations with Tim Heidecker, including *Tim and Eric Awesome Show, Great Job!,* and *Check It Out! With Dr. Steve Brule.* He directed, produced, and stars in Netflix's Emmy Award winning *Master of None.* Eric co-owns Las Jaras Wines, and runs one of Instagram's top food blogs. His first food book will be published in 2020.

IMPOSSIBLE CONTRIBUTORS

CAROLYN CHEN

Carolyn Chen is a Quality Assurance Technician at Impossible Foods, working on product quality assurance at the company's production facility in Oakland, California. She has a B.S. in Food Science and Technology with a minor in Nutrition Sciences from U.C. Davis. At work, she is known for having a huge appetite (and general love of food). In her spare time, she enjoys honing her food photography skills and working on arts and crafts.

JEN SHIU

An Associate Scientist at Impossible Foods, Jen Shiu joined the company in 2011 as one of the first employees. Jen earned a B.S. in Biochemistry and Molecular Biology from Rice University and an M.S. in Food Science at U.C. Davis. A food scientist by day, she is a pie-baking rock climber by nights and weekends. Her Thai-Chinese roots, by way of Texas, inspire her cooking sensibilities.

LAURA KLIMAN

Dr. Laura Kliman is a Senior Scientist on the Product Innovation team at Impossible Foods. Her research involves understanding flavor generation using plant-based ingredients. Laura received her Ph.D. in Organic Chemistry from Boston College and her bachelor's degree in Chemistry with a minor in Environmental Science from Boston University. Laura's dedication to environmental sustainability started at a young age and inspired her work with the Sierra Club and MASSPIRG. Her volunteer work includes teaching green chemistry to K-12 students.

MARJORIE MUNNEKE

Marjorie Munneke is a Senior R&D Manager on the Material and Texture team at Impossible Foods, where she started in 2015. She studied Food Science at North Carolina State University, and earned a Ph.D. in Chemistry from Victoria University of Wellington, New Zealand, where she developed a method to measure pico-Newton forces between emulsion droplets using laser-based "optical tweezers." She enjoys ceramics, baking for the Impossible Foods cake club, and going on long-distance hikes.

OLIVIA PEAR

A Research Associate at Impossible Foods, Olivia Pear works on material science and texture projects. She earned a B.S. in Chemical and Biomolecular Engineering at UC Berkeley, where she developed an interest in sustainable food and an ability to work long hours. She enjoys time spent outdoors—whether running or climbing—and is convinced this makes her a nicer person to be around. She dreams of one day living out of a van (electric, of course), to travel, and to escape Bay Area rents.

WINNIE YEOH

Winnie Yeoh is a Food Technologist on the Product Innovation team at Impossible Foods. Originally from Malaysia, she earned her B.S. in Food Science from the University of Wisconsin, Madison. Growing up in a multicultural country, Winnie was exposed to a wide variety of cuisines that helped shape her discerning palate. In her down time, she likes to tinker with dessert recipes and test them out on her housemates.

ACKNOWLEDGMENTS

Huge thanks to the team at Chronicle Books: Catherine Huchting, Beth Weber, Pamela Geismar, and Freesia Blizard, who guided us through the improbable (but Impossible) task of producing a full-fledged cookbook within six months.

Thanks particularly to the rockstar team of project editor Kim Laidlaw, writer Steve Siegelman, and master recipe tester Aralyn Beaumont. You embodied Impossible Foods' values of kindness and responsibility from the start.

We owe a debt of gratitude to the chefs and industry veterans who have been so supportive of the brand since we came out of stealth mode in 2016. Thank you to Andrei Soen, Brad Farmerie, Chris Cosentino, Douglas Keane, Eric Wareheim, Erik Drobey, Justin Cucci, Ken Oringer and Jamie Bissonnette, Kwame Onwuachi, Mary-Sue Milliken and Susan Feniger, May Chow, Michael Symon, Pinky Cole, Que Vinh Dang, Ricky Leung, Sarah Schafer, Tal Ronnen, and Tanya Holland.

The culinary minds and scientists at Impossible Foods have been integral to our achievements since the company was founded in 2011. Special shout-out to Head of Culinary J Michael Melton, and to Senior Flavor Scientist Laura Kliman, who was the biggest internal champion for this book. Thanks also to our employee contributors: Carolyn Chen, Jen Shiu, Marjorie Munneke, Olivia Pear, and Winnie Yeoh.

Our world-class, in-house creative team, led by Giselle Guerrero, nailed the unique look and feel of this cookbook, with support from our fantastic consultant Anne Kenady Smith and photographer Aubrie Pick. Special thank you to our Legal and Regulatory teams, including Tashir Lee, who saw the project from start to finish. Thanks also to our beautiful-in-side-and-out models Myra Nelson, Brenden Darby, Esther Cohn, Barflaan Tedoe, and Jotham Ndugga-Kabuye for bringing this book to life.

Master chef, philanthropist, and all-around taste guru Traci Des Jardins was the heart and soul of each page in this book—a true friend to everyone at Impossible Foods. Thanks for joining us on this exciting adventure!

This cookbook would not exist were it not for the unwavering efforts of the communications team's Swiss Army knife Rachel Soeharto, who took Laura Kliman's brilliant idea and got it through every stage of the process—from creative concept to chef recruiting to spell checking to publication to publicity, while keeping every internal and external stakeholder happily in the loop. The rest of us were consistently blown away by her never-ending zeal for this project.

Finally, everyone at Impossible Foods extends the biggest thanks to you, our friends and fans, for purchasing this cookbook and accelerating the shift to a sustainable food system—one delicious bite at a time.

INDEX